Chesterfield's Remarkable Women

Janet Murphy

First published in Great Britain in 2021 by
Bannister Publications Ltd
118 Saltergate, Chesterfield, Derbyshire S40 1NG
Copyright © Janet Murphy
ISBN: 978-1-909813-74-8

Typeset in Palatino

Printed and bound in Great Britain

This book was self-published by Bannister Publications.
For more information on self-publishing visit:
www.bannisterpublications.com

Introduction

For much of the 20th century, Chesterfield was regarded as a male-dominated town. Employment was principally in mining and engineering. Although World War I gave women and girls a freedom they had never had before, after the war, little had changed. It was not until 1925, that the first woman councillor was elected, and there were few female councillors until recent times. However, the perception that the town was male-dominated overlooks the part played by women in the town's development, as they were co-opted onto council committees, served on the Borough Welfare Committee, were elected to the Board of Guardians for the Workhouse, ran the Chesterfield Settlement, organised charities, served as magistrates and taught in schools. With the exception of Blanche Eastwood (Eastwood Park), and Mary Swanwick (Mary Swanwick School), their names have been forgotten.

Chesterfield's Remarkable Women is dedicated to these women. It includes some of their stories and those of other women whose extraordinary achievements deserve to be remembered.

Who was the most remarkable of all? Arguably it was Violet Markham. She was years ahead of her time, and many thousands had cause to be grateful to her as she worked to improve the standard of education in Chesterfield. She founded the Settlement, which initially sought to improve the welfare of girls and young mothers and babies, but greatly extended its work. Although she became involved in national affairs, she never forgot her home town.

All proceeds from the sale of the book will go to Ashgate Hospicecare.

Acknowledgments

Most of the information has come from Ancestry, Find My Past, the National Archives, the British Newspaper Archive and the Chesterfield Local Studies Library; other sources are mentioned in the text. I am particularly grateful for the assistance given by the staff of Chesterfield Local Studies Library and Chesterfield Museum and Art Gallery.

Images are reproduced by courtesy of the following organisations.

Chesterfield Local Studies Library	p28, 44, 65
Chesterfield Local Studies Library/Derbyshire Times	p85, 87
Chesterfield Museum and Art Gallery	p3, 32, 40, 63, 74, 106, 118, 120
Friends of Spital Cemetery	p117
National Army Museum, London	p109
Picture the Past	p47
Robinson family	p81
Short Publishing Co. Ltd	p98
Wikipedia	p37, 76

Other images are from the author's own collection.

Contents

The names are those by which the individuals are best known

Katie Bacon 1896-1982	1
Olave St Clair Lady Baden-Powell 1889-1977	4
Emma Louise Bond 1864-1943	7
Barbara Castle 1910-2002	11
Marjorie Cowley 1891-1947	13
Blanche Eastwood 1874-1963	15
Anne Veronica 1891-1918 and Mary Ellen Fletcher 1889-1924	18
Isabel Foljambe 1563-1623	21
Elizabeth Freeman 1876-1942	23
Susanna Frith ?-1686	25
Florrie Green 1898-?	27
Phyllis Hanson 1910-1994	31
Charlotte Harrison 1828-1868	33
Rhoda Lucy Harrison 1892-1967	34
Hilda Hawes 1893-1974	36
Betty Heathfield 1927-2006	38
Dame Jennifer Jenkins 1921-2017	40
Sarah Johnson 1761-1831	42
Winifred 1876-1955 and Gladys Jones 1878-1953	46
Annie King 1870-1900	50
Susan Mallinson 1942-2016	54
Margaret Markham 1864-1936	56
Violet Markham 1872-1959	57
Emma Miller 1839-1917	65

Lady Mary Murray 1732-1765   69

Catherine Parry 1925-2009   73

Baroness Richardson of Calow 1938-   75

Hannah Roberts 1798-1867   77

Florence 1888-1976, Cecile Bradbury 1893-1965   79
and Dorothy Robinson 1895-1985

Susan Shentall 1934-1996   84

Elizabeth Simon 1933-2013   86

Hannah Smith 1856-1966   88

Jessie Smith 1886-?   89

Rose Smith 1891-1985   91

Margaret Stovin 1756-1846   95

Mary Swanwick 1841-1917   99

Rhoda Tattersall 1902-1993   102

Greta Walker 1898-1973   104

Dorothy Webster 1906-1997   107

Minnie Wheatcroft 1897-1973   108

Helen Mary Wilcockson 1906-2002   110

Marie Louise Wilkes 1859-1910   112
and Alice Stevens 1862-193-?

Susannah Williams 1873-1956   116

Mary Woodhead 1904-1978   119

Amy Wright 1825-1893   121

Katie Bacon 1896-1982

Katie Edith Bacon was born on 2 June 1896, the daughter of Henry and Maud Bacon. Henry was the manager of Cavendish Motors. When Katie was four, she began playing the piano with a family friend before having proper lessons. When she was nine, she began studying more seriously with John Frederick Staton, who was the organist and choir master at Chesterfield Parish Church. Her first known public appearance, when she was described as an accomplished juvenile pianist, was, somewhat surprisingly, as part of the musical interlude at the amateur featherweight wrestling championship at the Parish Church Gymnastic Club in May 1908, when she was just 11-years-old. The previous month she had been taken to a concert by the young English pianist Arthur Newstead at Chesterfield. After the concert she played for him and he praised her talent and musical promise. Newstead, who was 15 years older, had already given many recitals abroad. Katie's father received a letter from him saying that he had been thinking very much of Katie's remarkable talent. He wondered if he could be of any assistance to Katie or her father proffering advice concerning Katie's future training. He offered to give her training in London providing Mr Staton had no objection. She began studying with Arthur Newstead, travelling up to London twice a week for her lessons. The following November, she took part in a concert at the Assembly Rooms in the Market Hall arranged by the Church of England Men's Society to raise funds for St Augustine's Church (presumably the iron chapel before the present church was built).

Katie appeared in concerts in Chesterfield in 1912 and 1913, the last one being in October 1913 before she sailed to the USA for eight months to continue her studies, Newstead having been invited to join the piano faculty of the Peabody Conservatory in Baltimore. At some stage it was decided that Kathleen Bacon sounded better but, for the folk of Chesterfield, she remained 'Our Katie'.

Endeavouring to get over her homesickness, she determined to make the best of her opportunities in America. In 1914, she was back in England playing three concerts at the Steinway Hall, before returning to America to continue her studies. The following year Arthur and Katie announced their engagement and, on 29 May 1916, three days after her graduation from Peabody, they were married. The following year a daughter Joan was born.

Shortly afterwards Newstead accepted a teaching position at the Institute of Musical Art (now the Juilliard School) in New York. For a while he commuted back and forth from Baltimore to New York, but eventually the family settled in New York.

After her New York debut in November 1920, Katie appeared with several orchestras, including the New York Philharmonic, Toronto Symphony and Baltimore Symphony Orchestras. She returned to England in 1925/6 and performed seven concerts at different venues, which were broadcast, but she still found time to perform at the Picture House (now the Winding Wheel Theatre) in October 1925.

Katie was still a British subject. When she returned to Chesterfield for a visit in 1936, the *Derbyshire Times* gave some idea of what this involved: she had to pay poll tax each time she entered the United States and, when leaving, she had to pay her income tax up to date. Her broadcasting and concert engagements were so exacting that she didn't know until the last minute whether she could join the White Star liner *Scythia* in New York, or at Boston, its first port of call. It is not surprising that on this visit Katie needed a complete rest. Her daughter Joan was said to show signs of following in the footsteps of her parents, as she had already won two scholarships for music.

In June 1949, Katie stayed for a month with her invalid father, who had moved to Mansfield. However, she was able to visit her friends in Chesterfield, where she received a tumultuous reception after a recital on the new Bechstein grand pianoforte which had been bought for the Civic Theatre (now the Pomegranate).

Her father died before the end of the year.

Her husband died in 1952, and the Juilliard Summer School program ceased, but Katie remained connected with the faculty, until she retired in 1972. Her punishing schedule continued. In 1955, she temporarily directed the Piano Department of the Chautauqua School of Music in New York. In addition to a full teaching schedule, her responsibilities included two weekly master classes, 13 different recital programs and an appearance with the Chautauqua Symphony Orchestra. A past student of that time remembered her remarking: "Nice weather ... for ducks", on a wet Manhattan morning – she didn't forget her English roots.

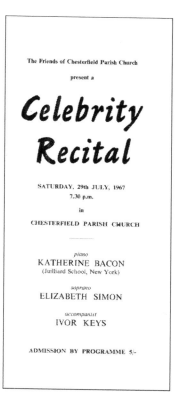

The Friends of Chesterfield Parish Church

present a

Celebrity Recital

SATURDAY, 29th JULY, 1967
7.30 p.m.

in

CHESTERFIELD PARISH CHURCH

piano
KATHERINE BACON
(Juilliard School, New York)

soprano
ELIZABETH SIMON

accompanist
IVOR KEYS

ADMISSION BY PROGRAMME 5/-

From 1930 to 1968, Katie lectured and performed at

universities and colleges throughout the United States as part of the Association of American Colleges Arts Program. In autumn 1966, a Far Eastern tour took her to Japan, Korea and Hong Kong for concerts, radio and television broadcasts, and lecture recitals.

Together with Elizabeth Simon (see Elizabeth Simon), she gave a recital for the Friends of Chesterfield Parish Church at the church on 29 July 1967, at the age of 70.

Katie Bacon died in a New York nursing home on 30 January 1982 at the age of 85.

See also:

https://www.lib.umd.edu/ipam/collections/katherine-bacon

Olave St Clair Lady Baden-Powell 1889-1977

In 1877, Brampton Brewery was sold at auction to Mr Harold Soames of Newark, bidding on behalf of Charles Chater, who was to be his partner. By 1881, Soames had moved to Stubbing Court with his brother Frederick. Two years later, he married Katherine Mary Hill at Holy Trinity, Paddington. 1889 was a momentous year for Harold as Chater withdrew from the partnership, leaving Harold as the sole proprietor of the brewery; Olave St Clair was born in February, joining a sister Ariol Edith and a brother Arthur George, and Harold Soames bought West House, West Bars, Chesterfield.

The house was described as a three-storey brick building of five bays, with the central three protruding slightly. There was a pediment on which a carving of a plum pudding represented hospitality. There were 16 bed and dressing rooms, and extensive grounds with a first-rate tennis ground, a kitchen garden, conservatory and vinery. Formal lessons were never popular with Olave, and she had a series of pets upon which she lavished her care and attention.

On the opposite side of West Bars was an area known as Maynard's meadows, leading down to the River Hipper. The land on the other side of the river had been purchased by the people of Chesterfield in order to lay out Queen's Park. Unfortunately for the family, this pleasant outlook didn't last very long as Maynard's meadows had been sold. In 1895, work started on the construction of the Lancashire, Derbyshire and East Coast Railway which opened in 1897, with the Market Place Station and marshalling yards directly opposite their home. West House was sold in April 1895, together with the contents, garden equipment and plants. Was Olave sorry to see the 80 Langshan and Minorca fowls sold?

The family moved to Renishaw Hall, which Harold Soames was renting from the Sitwell family. Olave's mother advertised for a 'thoroughly competent English or German governess for two girls aged seven and ten' to teach them music, drawing and German. The family didn't stay at Renishaw very long, as in June 1897, 'stove and greenhouse orchids, plants and ferns' were offered for sale. Their father sold the brewery in July 1897, as his health had deteriorated, and the family moved to the south of England. They moved several times before eventually settling at Gray Rigg, a substantial Victorian property near Poole Harbour. This would have suited Olave, who was keen on outdoor sports including tennis, swimming, and canoeing.

In 1912, on a voyage aboard the *Arcadian* to New York via the Caribbean, she met Lord Robert Baden-Powell. Despite the disparity in their ages – she was 23 and he was 55 – the couple were engaged and married very quietly in November the same year. They had one son and two daughters.

Olave Baden-Powell returned to Chesterfield on 4 June 1914, when she inspected 250 Boy Scouts in the grounds of Rose Hill, only a few yards from her old home, and presented a new flag to the 2nd Chesterfield Scout Troop. Speaking at the rally and fête, she said that it had been 20 years since she had left Chesterfield, and she hoped it wouldn't be another 20 years before she returned again. Olave was made Chief Guide in 1918, and World Chief Guide in 1930, shortly before she visited Chesterfield to open the Girl Guides' headquarters on St Margaret's Drive, before inspecting the Guides on the Recreation Ground. The editor of the *Derbyshire Times* was quite impressed with her. 'Lady Baden-Powell has the knack of getting on good terms with the girls at once, and all were delighted with the way she inspected them and the common-sense and telling remarks she addressed to them'.

West House was still standing then, but it was demolished in 1935, before she visited Chesterfield again on 13 November 1936 to address a public meeting at the Chesterfield Girls' High School on the importance of guiding, after attending a gathering of Guides at Bradbury Hall. In 1938, Olave moved to Kenya with her husband who died there in 1941. She returned to Britain, and visited Chesterfield once more in May 1943, when she reviewed the Brownies at the Girls' High School, before having tea at Elder Yard Chapel, and then taking the salute at a march past of the Guides at the football ground. She expressed delight to be in her native town, where she had such a happy time as a girl: "Your town is very dear to me and always will be."

In 1951, Olave spent three days touring Derbyshire. In Chesterfield, she met the Brownies in St James Hall, took the salute at a march past of Guides, attended a service at the Parish Church and, at a meeting in the evening, she addressed an invited audience which included members of the general public involved in education and youth services, and representatives of firms employing girls.

Olive Lady Baden-Powell died at Bramley, Surrey in 1977.

Emma Louise Bond 1864-1943

Emma Louise Baker was born at North Shields in 1864. At the time of the 1871 census she was a boarder at a school in North Shields. Ten years later, she was living with her grandmother Isabella Hills in Sunderland.

In January 1891, Kenneth Bond preached his first sermon at Swadlincote Baptist Church. It was said that he had lately been 'employed in the vicinity of Holborn, London as a Missioner in the Forward Movement'. This is probably where he met Emma Louise Baker, who was lodging in Clerkenwell with other deaconesses. The couple married at North Shields the same year and, whilst living in Swadlincote, they had four children, Kenneth Hills, Frederick Noel, Clifford and Cedric Meyer. A fifth child, Annie Louise, was born in Desford, Leicestershire. Kenneth Bond became a minister of the Free Christian Church, moving to Chesterfield's Elder Yard Unitarian Chapel in 1913.

Two of their sons enlisted in WWI; Kenneth joined the Sherwood Foresters, Noel left the Grammar School in August 1915 to join the Sportsmen's Battalion of the Royal Fusiliers. He was killed in August 1916. Addressing a meeting on the third anniversary of the beginning of the war, Emma Louise said: "This war has done something for the women and girls – it has given them a freedom they have never had before."

Emma Louise soon became very involved with welfare work in the town. She ran the Sunday school at the Chapel, helped with the Settlement (see Violet Markham) and was a member of the British Women's Temperance Association, the Chesterfield District Nursing Association and the Civic Guild. She was the only woman member of the Food Control Committee, established in August 1917, and she worked with the Borough Welfare Committee. She was also an articulate public speaker. All of this stood her in good stead when she was chosen to stand as a Labour candidate in Holmebrook Ward in the 1920 municipal election, the only woman to stand in the election. Her speech was reproduced in the *Derbyshire Courier* of 2 October 1920.

'Mrs Bond's Life on £100 a Year.

Mrs Kenneth Bond had a cordial reception."I feel grateful", she said, "to find that the critics approve of me. (Laughter.) I am rather surprised that they do, because they might have thought, 'What does she know? She has only just come into Chesterfield. She is an interloper. She has not lived here all her life. What do strangers know about this grand old town of ours? (Laughter.) Why should they criticise any conditions of the town?' They may say, too, that I am new to the Labour movement. They would be quite right. I am a chicken in the movement, because I have not been in it very long. But I can say this: I have very great sympathy for the workers. I do feel that I am one of them, because I am a worker myself. I think it is only a woman who has been through the mill, striven and struggled to make the best of circumstances, who can understand the hardships of other women. When I was a girl little did I think it would be my lot to work in the slums of London and see the conditions under which some women have to work. I do not think that it is any great secret that parsons and curates are not well paid. When I was a young wife there were articles in the papers on 'Gloriously happy on £100 a year' and 'Passing rich on £100 a year'. There were many curates and ministers' wives who did live on £100 year and I was one of them. You will understand that my lot was not one of the easiest. We did feel rich when there were only two of us, but when there were five children as well and only £130 or £140 year coming in we did not feel so rich. It was not easy for me to keep a servant. I am here as a woman on a Labour platform to plead for the homes of the women. I have been told that a woman's place is at home, and that is where a woman ought to stay. I say that if the men don't alter these conditions – and they have not altered them – then women will have to stir them up. (Hear, hear.) I am sorry there is no other woman candidate for the Council. I don't know how I shall feel when I get amongst all the men. I am sorry that other women have backed out, and are not willing to stand, but if I do get in and do any good perhaps they will come out next time. (Hear, hear.)

I am not going to say that Chesterfield is any worse than other places. I don't say it is, but it is bad enough. One of the beautiful things in Chesterfield is that wherever you go you can see the country outside.

You women who have husbands that go to work all day are very fortunate. (Laughter.) One place where we lived Mr Bond used the back kitchen for his study, and the door did not fit very well. When he was trying to make a sermon or read a book he heard the baby every time it cried. He said: "This is no good for me" and went to the vestry at the chapel. Then for the first time in my life I had a man out of the house from breakfast time to dinner time. (Laughter.)'

She was narrowly defeated, but was co-opted onto the Maternity and Child Welfare Committee. Unfortunately, just before the election, Kenneth Bond had announced that he was moving to St Helens, Lancashire the following year, and this may have influenced the result. The couple left in April 1921, taking with them a tea service and a silver-plated cake stand. They served at Mexborough and Bolton upon Dearne, before moving south to Moretonhampstead and Newton Abbot in Devon.

Elder Yard Unitarian Chapel. The gates and railings were designed by Clifford Bond.

Their son Clifford qualified as an architect in Chesterfield. Kenneth and his wife returned to Chesterfield in 1935 for the marriage of Clifford to Barbara Johnson.

They retired to Ringwood in Hampshire, where Kenneth Bond died in May 1943, and Emma Louise in November 1943.

Barbara Castle 1910-2002

Little can be said about Barbara Castle's time in Chesterfield, as she only lived in Chesterfield for a few months. Much has been written elsewhere about her career in politics, so only a brief outline is included here.

Barbara Annie Betts was born in October 1910, the daughter of Frederick Betts and his wife Annie Rebecca, née Ferrand. Her father was a high-ranking tax inspector, which meant that he moved frequently, and also exempted him from service in WWI. Although her parents had been born in Coventry, they moved from the rural area of East Dereham in Norfolk (where her elder sister Marjorie was born) to industrial Chesterfield, in about 1908. They lived at Mancroft on Derby Road, in close proximity to Bryan Donkin's and the Tube Works. According to the 1911 census, the property had seven rooms. After the family moved in May 1911, it was offered to let and was described as 'a semi-detached villa with a bathroom and wc and large and lofty rooms with every convenience'. Her brother Tristram Frederick was also born in Chesterfield.

In May 1910, considerable interest was raised in the town over an inquest into the body of an old man found in the canal. It was claimed that he had been refused outdoor relief from the Workhouse, and the Relieving Officer was heavily criticised. Among the angry letters to the *Derbyshire Courier* about Poor Law Relief, there was one from Annie, demanding an enquiry into the case. As a civil servant, Frederick would not been allowed to get involved. Also, in 1910, James Haslam was re-elected as a Labour MP to represent Chesterfield. This would have pleased Barbara's parents, who were known to be Labour Party supporters. Frederick was a member of the Fabian Society in the town, and in February 1911 he delivered a paper on town planning to the Chesterfield Trades Council. The same month, he produced the play *Silver Box* by John Galsworthy at the Market Hall. According to the *Derbyshire Courier*, it is 'a play which treats boldly the inequalities of justice which society metes out to rich and poor': Frank and Annie were 'conspicuous for their acting'.

By 1922, the family was living in Bradford, where Barbara attended Bradford Girls' Grammar School, before obtaining a degree at St Hugh's College, Oxford. She moved to London, where she became a member of St Pancras Borough Council in 1937. Together with Michael Foot, she founded *The Tribune*, and during the war she was a journalist for the *Daily Mirror*. She married Ted Castle in 1944 and, a year later, was elected MP for Blackburn (1945-79) – not because she had any connection with Blackburn, but reputedly because the women of Blackburn insisted in having a woman candidate.

In May 1960, she was the guest speaker at the Chesterfield Labour Party Dinner.

As Minister of Transport (1965-8), she introduced seat belts and breathalysers, and made permanent the 70 mph speed limit with the aim of reducing deaths resulting from road accidents. During her period in office, the M1 was opened east of Chesterfield in 1967. She also presided over the Beeching railway cuts. As First Secretary of State for Employment (1968-70), she introduced the Equal Pay Act in 1970. As Secretary of State for Health and Social Services (1974-6), she oversaw the introduction of the Child Benefit Act of 1975, which reformed child benefit allowances, allowing benefits for the first child, and the payment of the allowance to the mothers. She also refined the Invalid Care Allowance (1976) for single women and others who had to give up full-time jobs to care for invalids. When she left Parliament in 1979, she was elected to the European Parliament from 1979-89. In 1990, she was created a life peer, 'Baroness Castle of Blackburn'.

A redhead, she always took great care with her appearance, and had a wig to use if she was unable to keep her Friday appointment with her hairdresser. She was an articulate public speaker. The reforms she introduced led to her being chosen in 2016 as one of the *Women's Hour's* seven women of the last 70 years who had the biggest impact on women's lives.

She died in 2002. Although she spent only a short time in Chesterfield, her actions had a profound effect on the women of Chesterfield.

Marjorie Cowley 1891-1947

WWI changed many people's lives, but 23-year-old Marjorie Cowley's life changed in a way that she could not have anticipated. She was born on 7 July 1891, the youngest daughter of Benjamin Cowley, who was employed in the Duke of Devonshire's estate office, and his wife Mary Emma. She had an older brother and two older sisters. Her father died in 1907 at the comparatively young age of 48, leaving the family in straitened circumstances.

Marjorie attended the Chesterfield Girls' High School from May 1897 until July 1907. The school log book for this period has not survived, but there is an entry in a later log book for Marjorie's return in May 1910, as a pupil teacher in the kindergarten. Her fees would have been £9, but she had a reduction of £3, because of help given in the kindergarten as a student teacher. When she left in April 1911, she was intending to be a governess in a kindergarten. Marjorie attended the funeral of Miss Wilkes in December 1910, when she was described as a 'past student'.

Nothing more is known about Marjorie until 26 February 1918, when she married Howard Whittall at Ormskirk in Lancashire. Howard was an Australian soldier who had enlisted in June 1915. He was transferred to Egypt for training, before embarking for France in March 1916. On 2 January 1918, he was admitted to hospital with trench fever, and was transferred to the Canadian General Hospital at Étaples. He remained there until 20 January, when he boarded the Hospital Ship *Newhaven* on his way to the Grange Hospital, Southport. This is where, presumably, he met Marjorie, or 'Bab' as she preferred to be known, who was a nurse there. Her headdress shows she was a trained nurse.

Margery at Grange Hospital

The Grange was a large house in Roe Lane, Southport, owned by Major Fleetwood-Hesketh, who offered it as a military hospital. By the end of 1915, it had five wards behind the permanent building, two of which were open air. Together with the Woodlands, another private house, it operated as one of the biggest Voluntary Aid Detachment (VAD) hospitals in the country run by the Order of St John.

At some stage, Howard was

diagnosed as suffering from pyelonephritis, an inflammation of the kidney tissue and pelvis, which was caused by a bacterial infection transferred by lice, following on from the trench fever. He was transferred to the First Australian Auxiliary Hospital at Harefield, Middlesex. Inevitably, this separated the couple, but Howard was granted a furlough from 25 February until 11 March, and the couple were married at Ormskirk by Revd W Platt. Howard had to report to the Australian Imperial Force Headquarters in London; from there he was sent to Hurdcott in Wiltshire for the next stage in his convalescence. Here it was decided that, as he was not going to be fit for active service for at least six months, he should be transferred to Number 2 Command at Weymouth, where soldiers unfit for service were prepared for repatriation to Australia. Although Marjorie took lodgings in Weymouth, she was soon on her own again, as Howard was transported to Australia aboard the troop transport *Essex*, leaving Liverpool on 13 June and arriving in Australia on 1 August 1918. Marjorie followed at a later date, as a nurse on HMAT *Marathon*. She never returned to England.

Howard was formally discharged from the army on 4 March 1919. He purchased a 23-acre farm on the outskirts of Sydney, where he reared horses, cattle and especially pigs, for which he won prizes. Marjorie retained her connection with the Red Cross. In 1946, Howard sold up due to ill health, but sadly the couple did not have a peaceful retirement, as Marjorie died in June 1947, and Howard six months later.

Blanche Eastwood 1874-1963

Susie Blanche Eastwood (also known as Blanche) was the daughter of Edward Isaac Eastwood and Susannah Blanche, née Bush. She was born in 1874, when her parents were living on

Sheffield Road, Chesterfield. The family then moved to Market
Harborough, where Ada Moore, Edward, and Joseph were born;
Mary Telford was born at Loughborough. Their father was an
engineer, and in 1884 he was sent to Russia on business where
he died aged just 33 years. A contributory factor to his death was
thought to be his liking for alcohol, and other members of the
family became strongly teetotal. His unfortunate widow was
pregnant, and another son George Richard was born after she
moved back to Long Eaton, where she had been born, until 1925,
when she moved back to Chesterfield.

Following her father's death, Susie Blanche was brought up
by her grandparents, Edward and Abigail, at Tapton Villa, which
was eventually demolished in 1938 to make way for an office
extension and wagon repair workshops at the Eastwood Wagon
Works on Brimington Road. She attended the Chesterfield
Science and Art classes, where she won a prize for freehand in
1890.

A tall lady with black hair and blue eyes, Blanche was
mayoress when her uncle, George Albert, was mayor between
1905 and 1907. As George's father had died the year before, and
his sister Josephine married in 1911, George Albert moved into
Brambling House on Hady Hill taking Blanche with him. She
remained beside him and cared for him until he died in 1934.
The family worshipped at the Independent Chapel on Rose Hill
(now the United Reformed Church). Four years after his death,
she donated the 'Samaritan' stained glass window in his
memory. In 1956, she paid for the Eastwood Memorial Hall,
attached to the church to commemorate the long association of
the family with the church; it was opened by her friend Violet
Markham.

In 1913, Blanche was presented with the key to open the
gates of Eastwood Park, Hasland, as a memorial to her

grandfather Edward. The land for the park had been given by George Albert Eastwood.

Violet Markham was the first woman to be elected to the town council, following a by-election in April 1925, and Blanche joined her the following November, when she was elected as an Independent in Hasland Ward, a position she held until 1934. The same year, she took over the management of the Wagon Works after the death of George Albert. She also moved to the smaller Brambling Cottage, where she remained until her death.

The family grave at Spital Cemetery where Blanche Eastwood is buried. Note also the record of the death of her father.

She served as a magistrate for nearly 30 years, for much of the time on the Juvenile Panel. She served as a member of the Board of Management of the Royal Hospital[1], as a leader in the Girl Guide movement in Chesterfield, and President of the Ragged School. She lived a very busy life, serving the inhabitants of the town to the full.

When she died in 1963, there was a private service at her home, before she was interred with other members of the family at Spital Cemetery. She was said to be the richest woman in the town at the time, leaving £¾ million on her death.

Anne Veronica 1891-1918 and Mary Ellen Fletcher 1889-1924

Annie and Mary Ellen were daughters of Daniel Fletcher, a coalminer, and his wife Mary. They were born at Ripley. The family moved to Chesterfield and, in 1901, they were living in Barrack Square off Packers Row. The children were James (17), Charles (15), Annie (10), Lucy (9), Catherine (7), Winnifred (5) and Maria (3), all born at Ripley, and John (8 months) born in Chesterfield. Mary Ellen (12) was staying next door, and Margaret Ann (20) was a general servant at the Red Lion on Vicar Lane.

By 1911, Daniel and his wife were living at Spital Gardens off Alexandra Road, Spital, but unfortunately the houses were missed from the census. However, Margaret Ann was housekeeper to Rev George Bradley, a Roman Catholic Priest, at St Wilfrid's Sheffield. Also living there were Mary and Honora, aged two and a half, possibly their sister, making 11 children in the family. Annie was a domestic servant in the household of Andrew Leonard, a Catholic priest at St Peter's Doncaster. The family were Catholics.

After three years training in Bradford, Annie joined East

1. Chesterfield and North Derbyshire District Hospital became the Chesterfield and North Derbyshire District Royal Hospital in 1918 and thereafter was commonly referred to as the Royal Hospital.

Leeds War Hospital as a nurse in the Territorial Force Nursing Service, on 7 May 1915. Unfortunately, her matron did not have a high opinion of her, describing her as needing constant supervision, and saying that she did not appear to be able to work harmoniously with her fellow nurses. Nevertheless, when King George V visited the hospital in September 1915, he congratulated Annie on her bandaging. At some stage, Annie became Anne Veronica – perhaps there had been more than one Annie Fletcher.

In February 1917, her health began to deteriorate and, in April, a medical board recommended that she should be given three months leave with pay. Also as she had developed TB, sanatorium treatment should be considered. After a delay whilst treatment was organised, she left the service on 11 June 1917 with a gratuity of £15 14s 4d, being admitted to Walton Sanatorium on 27 June. She was awarded a Silver War Badge, as the 'disability was caused while on duty in a Military Hospital during the recent war'. Sadly, her health continued to deteriorate and eventually she returned home, where she died on 12 March 1918. After a requiem mass at the Church of the Annunciation, Anne Veronica was buried at Spital Cemetery.

All the sisters were present at the funeral with the exception of her sister Mary. According to the *Derbyshire Courier* report, Mary 'did service as "the lady of the lamp" at the Dardanelles, and is at present in Palestine', but, according to the *Derbyshire Times*, 'she went to Malta three years ago but is now with the British Army in Palestine'. There is a medal roll entry in the National Archives for a 'Mary Fletcher', who was a member of the Queen Alexandra's Imperial Nursing Service Reserve (QAIMNSR). This would appear to be the right person, as the record shows that she entered Theatre of War 3 on 21 October 1915. Theatre of War 3 included Egypt and Palestine.

Early in 1915, Mary would have applied to join the QAIMNS, the military nurses. When WWI started, there were just 297 QAIMNS nurses, who were expected to be 'trained, single, over 25 and of a high social status'. On the outbreak of war, restrictions had to be relaxed because of the demand for professionally-qualified nurses, and thousands of fit, usually single, middle and upper-class nurses, who worked professionally in civilian hospitals, were recruited into the QAIMNS Reserve. One of these was Mary. She would have signed up for service 'for as long as her services are required during the present emergency'. First of all, she set sail for Malta. The first nurses arrived there on 7 May 1915; at the end of the month there were 219; and by the end of September there were 567 sisters. The rapid expansion was necessary because of the Gallipoli campaign, which resulted in thousands of casualties of different nationalities. Most new nurses arriving, like Mary, would have been without experience of the work of military hospitals, and they had to adapt rapidly to the routines, and irregular meals and sleep. As more medical staff arrived, Mary was posted to Egypt, which, unlike Malta, was classed as a theatre of war. She arrived on 21 October 1915. Co-incidentally, she was in Egypt at the same time as Howard Whittall (who later married Marjorie Cowley) and John Harrison (see Ruth Harrison). At least Howard would be more accustomed to the heat than Mary. She could have been posted to one of the hospital ships caring for the sick and wounded men evacuated from the Gallipoli campaign, or to one of the hospitals in Egypt.[2]

The Gallipoli campaign was comparatively short, with the major offensive being in August 1915, and the evacuation between December 1915 and January 1916. Attention then turned to the Sinai Peninsula, and eventually Palestine, where the war effectively ended in September 1918.

2. For a graphic account of experiences aboard a hospital ship operating from Egypt see The Nightingale Tradition in The Imperial War Museum Book of the First World War by Malcolm Brown. ISBN 978-0-283999-46-8

Mary joined as a staff nurse and was promoted to sister. When she applied to join QAIMNSR, she could never have imagined the experiences she would undergo before she returned to England. Nothing more is known of her until her possible death in Liverpool in 1924 at the age of just 35.

Isabel Foljambe 1563-1623

Isabel Wray was born at Glentworth, Lincolnshire, the daughter of Christopher Wray and his wife Anne, née Girlington. Wray was the Lord Chief Justice at the time of Elizabeth I. Isabel had a younger sister Frances, and a brother William, who was a staunch Puritan. In the late 16th and early 17th centuries, Puritans maintained that, after the Reformation, the Church of England was not fully purged of Roman Catholic practices, which the Puritans sought to remove.

Isabel married Godfrey Foljambe of Walton Hall around 1587. She too was a Puritan. She became involved in an exorcism case involving Katherine Wright of Whittington, who was said to be possessed by the devil. Isabel also supported young men through university, usually Cambridge, before she sought to place them in suitable parishes.

Godfrey died in 1595 aged just 37. As there were no children, he left the greater part of his estate to his wife for life. About 1598, Isabel married Sir William Bowes. She remained at Walton, as Sir William was much involved in negotiations on the Scottish borders.

Some members of the clergy were deprived of their livings for holding nonconformist views. In 1606, Isabel, now Lady Bowes, hosted a conference of leading Puritans at her house in Coventry, where they debated whether or not they should separate from the Church of England. A split developed with some clergy remaining with the Church of England; others decided to leave, effectively establishing a nonconformist tradition in church life. Some Puritans decided to leave for the Netherlands, and ultimately, for New England. Isabel seems to have continued her support for Puritan clergy, including those who lost their livings as the pressure for conformity increased.

Sir William died in 1611, and Isabel married Lord John Darcy, before she died at Aldwark near York, the property of Sir Francis Foljambe. There is an effigy of her on Godfrey Foljambe's tomb in Chesterfield Parish Church.

For further information see:

https://www.pilgrimsandprophets.co.uk/historical/two-sisters-and-the-puritan-revolution/

Isabel's effigy in Chesterfield Parish Church

Elizabeth Freeman 1876-1942

Sarah Elizabeth Freeman was the daughter of Mary and George Freeman, whose marriage was registered in Chesterfield in 1874. At the time of the 1881 census, Sarah Elizabeth was living with her grandparents, Francis and Jane Hall, and her brother John Francis Hall, aged seven, on Mansfield Road, Hasland. John's birth had been registered as John Francis Freeman Hall, so it was likely that George Freeman was his father. There was also a sister Jane, but neither Jane nor their mother Mary can be found in the 1881 census, nor can any birth of Jane be traced for certain. Mary and George had parted company. Mary left for the United States with her young children. The family lived in New York. Jane became a notable artist; John Francis Freeman became a typesetter for New York newspapers and a leader in the printers' union.

According to family sources, Elizabeth visited England in 1894, when a surviving diary reveals her as a moody and bored young woman, animated only by instances of injustice, and Salvation Army meetings both in England and the United States. She returned to England with her mother in 1905, ostensibly to study social conditions, and this time things were very different. She saw a policeman beating up a woman and, when she ran to help, she too was arrested. Presumably this had been at a suffragette protest. Whilst she was in prison, she learned about the suffragette cause and the militant tactics of the Women's Social and Political Union. As well as selling the WSPU publication *Votes for Women*, she became an impressive and articulate public speaker – sometimes sharing the stage with the Pankhursts and Mrs Pethick Lawrence. She was leading open-air meetings in June 1909, and frequently attended drawing-room meetings. In July 1910, two processions, one from the east and the other from the west, converged on Hyde Park, where 150 speakers addressed a crowd of up to 20,000 from 40 platforms, one of which was in the charge of Elizabeth. On 17 June 1911, she was the leader of the International Contingent, which took part in a great march (estimated to be 40,000 women from all walks of life) to a meeting at the Albert Hall. According to the family, she was arrested at least eight times and was imprisoned in Holloway jail.

She was back in the United States by February 1912, where a group of suffragettes banded together to perform suffrage plays. She continued her militant activities, being involved in the New York garment makers' strike, the Colorado miners' strike, and the Suffrage March of 1913 to Woodrow Wilson's inauguration. After this she became a civil rights worker. She was opposed to the United States entering the war.

Elizabeth was upset at what she saw as the collapse of the militant suffragette movement in England as, on the outbreak of war, the campaigners scattered, some to war work; some to pacifist activities; others seeking election to the Municipal and County Councils; others to the dull grind of factory work; and some just dropped out of sight. She felt that the suffering of the women in the militant movement from 1905 to 1914 seemed a waste of energy, when they accepted, what she regarded as the meagre crumb of comfort of women over 30 years of age, with minimum property qualifications, being given the Parliamentary vote – rather than all women.

Having been on hunger strike at least twice it is not surprising that Elizabeth suffered from ill health. She owned an antique store in Massachusetts from 1925 until 1937, when she moved to California for health reasons. This is where she died in 1942.

See also: http://www.elizabethfreeman.org/london.php

Susanna Frith ?-1686

The founder of the Society of Friends or Quakers, George Fox, came to Chesterfield in 1650. Quakers were easily identifiable in the town. The men wore brown suits, gaiters, and broad-brimmed hats; the women wore silver grey gowns, plain shawls, and coal scuttle hats.

The early Quakers suffered much persecution, partly because some of them refused to pay tithes to the Established Church, and partly because of the 1664 Conventicle Act, which declared that it was illegal for more than five people to gather together for religious worship not using the Book of Common Prayer. In 1666, George Fox visited Derbyshire again, reporting that 'some Friends were afraid of the constables coming in for they had great persecution in these parts'. Susanna (or Susan) Frith, spoke out against the persecution of Quakers in the town by the local justices. When Ellen Fretwell had her goods removed on the orders of Justice Godfrey Clarke, she went to the Sessions Court, where other justices were sympathetic and ordered their return. Susanna 'was moved of the Lord to tell him (Clarke) that if he continued in his persecuting, the Lord would execute his plagues upon him'. He reportedly went home, 'fell distracted and died'. This is unlikely to have happened, as he died in 1670, but Susanna could hardly have endeared herself to him. She also declared:

"This is my testimoney concerning tithes that since the Lord convinced mee of his everlasting truth I have not to pay tithes to any priest or Steepellhouse sesments to any but have borne my testimony against all such practises both in word and writeing and in suffering imprisonment under priest Coope of Chesterfield and my goods have beene taken for not paying to the Steepellhouse severall times as for the tithe of my corne I never tooke it of any but I have ordered to gett it in before the tithe men came and I never left them any."

This was copied into the Chesterfield Monthly meeting minute book, which began in 1691. Coope (or Coupe) was the vicar of Chesterfield from 1664-1683.

There is no early record of a Quaker marriage of John and Susanna. However, when Susanna died in 1686, she was recorded as the widow of John Frith, who might have been John Frith, dyer, who died in 1667. The couple had at least four children, John, Joseph, Susanna and Stephen.

Joseph Besse recorded the persecutions in *A collection of the sufferings of the people called Quakers*. It records the punishments meted out to John and Susanna. John had his horse taken away for failing to pay three shillings for tithes and an Easter offering. In 1663, he was imprisoned for failing to pay his Easter offering. Later in the year, he and three others were taken out of a meeting and sent to the House of Correction on South Street in Chesterfield. In May 1665, a meeting was broken up on the orders of the Mayor. Most of the people were driven out of town, but three were committed to the House of Correction for three months and Susanna, taken when out of the meeting, was also sent to the same place. In September the same year, justices took the names of people attending a meeting at Wingerworth – 31 of them were sent to the House of Correction of whom 13, including John, were to be detained there until the next Sessions. Clearly the Conventicle Act was being applied with enthusiasm by the justices. Susanna can hardly have been unaffected by punishments meted out to John.

About 1668, John and Susanna were excommunicated because of their failure to attend public worship. This was too late for John, who died in 1667 – most likely his incarceration in the House of Correction, which was unlikely to be a pleasant experience, contributed to his death. Susanna was left a widow, but the persecution didn't stop. In 1670, she was fined £13 7s for being at a meeting at the house of John Holmes (fined £30), when most of the others were fined £1 or less. She was fined twice more before her death.

The heaviest penalties came when individuals were punished for not attending church. In 1685, the Sherriff's deputy demanded £120 as John junior had not attended the parish church for six months. When he refused to pay, 30 sheep, four kine, two foals and three horses were driven away. Unfortunately for the authorities, the sheep and cattle were put in a pasture which was inadequately fenced, and they escaped and made their way home.

The Toleration Act of 1689 allowed dissenters to meet and worship. The houses of John and Joseph, the sons of Susanna, were licensed for meetings. They still refused to pay tithes. It was the next generation of John and Joseph who were committed to the common gaol.

In 1675, she was witness at the marriage of her daughter Susanna. She and her son John were also witnesses to the marriage of Joseph Frith. Susanna Frith, widow of John Frith senior, was buried in 1686. She died before the Meeting House (since demolished) was opened in 1697.

Florrie Green 1898-?

Florrie Green was the daughter of William Henry Green, a miner, and his wife Eliza Ann. At the time of the 1911 census, the family was living on Derby Road at Birdholme. Florrie had two older brothers, two other brothers having died young, and two younger sisters. After leaving school, Florrie went to work as a

weaver at Robinson & Sons' Wheatbridge Works. Her sister
Nellie joined her there.

Women's football became increasingly popular in 1917 and
many teams were formed by munition workers. On New Year's
Day 1917, a football match was played at the Recreation Ground,
Saltergate. A crowd of 3,000 were attracted by the teams
composed of women working at Bryan Donkin and Chesterfield
Tube Works. As an exhibition of football, the game was hardly a
success, but it caused much amusement. The ground was heavy;
the players were soon spattered with mud; they found it difficult
to kick the ball very far. They were somewhat ignorant of the
rules, and tackling their opponents often meant pulling their
shirts. The funds raised went to the hospital, and tobacco for the
local soldiers.

Thought to be the Robinson & Sons' football team

1917 saw an effort by the traders of the town to raise money
for the Chesterfield & North Derbyshire Hospital, and one of the
events was a match between women from the Wheatbridge
Works and the Holmebrook Works of Robinson & Sons, who
were the biggest employers of women in the town. This time, the

game was of a higher standard with Holmebrook winning 1-0. The Wheatbridge team included Florrie and her sister Nellie. A few weeks later, Wheatbridge got their revenge, winning 3-1 with Florrie scoring two goals. This time, the money raised went towards the Brampton Moor Soldiers' fund.

Although there were several local teams playing, an attempt by a Mr William Airey to organise a competition between the sides was not very successful, with only four teams entering. The first semi-final was between Wheatbridge Works and Markham Works. It was a somewhat one-sided affair, with Wheatbridge winning 14-0 and Florrie scoring eight goals. The other semi-final was much closer, with Holmebrook beating Bryan Donkin 3-1. On Easter Saturday, an estimated 4,000 people watched the final at the Recreation Ground. This was a close-fought game with Wheatbridge winning 2-1. The Wheatbridge side was said to be showing the benefit of the training they had received from Taylor, a former Chesterfield FC player. The receipts for the competition were £246 – expenses included £23 amusement tax, which seems a bit harsh, as the money raised was for the hospital, and tobacco for the soldiers.

Wheatbridge continued their successful ways. They defeated Barrow Hill 9-1 and Staveley 8-1. The latter was their seventh match, of which they had only lost the first one. They had scored 42 goals, of which their captain Florrie Green had scored an amazing 25.

During the summer, Chesterfield Ladies' Football Club was formed. In October, they played a demonstration game against Ripley at the Ratcliffe Gate ground of Mansfield Town. This time, the star of the side was said to be redheaded Violet Watts, 'a tall girl with any amount of energy'. In December, they met the Ministry of Inspections Department, Nottingham, in a match on behalf of the local Sporting Club's effort in aid of the Duchess of Portland's Nottingham Home for Paralysed Soldiers and Sailors. The *Derbyshire Courier* for 22 December 1917 described the Chesterfield side as a club, which 'won many matches and possess a powerful wonderful goal-scoring centre-forward in Miss F Green, a big girl exactly built for the position, with a good turn of speed and the gift of marksmanship. The Derbyshire side has been well coached and has, by this time, acquired quite a useful knowledge of how football should be played both in attack and in defence.' Chesterfield won 6-0.

There were few reports of women's football in 1918. Partly, this was because it was no longer a novelty, and partly because fewer women were employed in munitions work. Men, who were no longer fit for active service, were being employed instead, and later fewer women were required as the war effort was being wound down. Less affected than most, were the weavers of Robinson & Sons Wheatbridge Works, as weaving was traditionally women's work. At the end of August, a match was arranged between the ladies of Robinson & Sons and disabled men from the Comrades of the Great War Association. Clearly, it was an entertaining game, as each side scored seven goals. Although the names of the men who scored were given the names of the female scorers were not! At the end of September, the same side met the Mid-Derbyshire Munition Workers in a match to raise funds for the YWCA.

Women footballers did not find favour with the Football Association, and in 1921, women were banned from playing football, as it was deemed a most unsuitable game, which was too much for a woman's physical frame.

Nothing more is known of Florrie.

Phyllis Annie Hanson 1910-1994

Phyllis Hanson was the daughter of Fred Hanson and his wife Lizzie. Fred was a saddler and harness maker. Possibly, he worked for William Bennett on Beetwell Street, as he bought Bennett's business in 1924. In 1939, the business moved to Cavendish Street, where Fred and Phyllis ran the business until Fred's death in 1952. Phyllis then took over, selling the business 13 years later.

Phyllis attended Chesterfield Girls' High School from 1923-8. In 1991, Phyllis attended a reunion of the old girls of school (later renamed St Helena), at which those attending were invited to record their life after school, and memories of the school. Phyllis merely recorded, 'Worked. Hobbies drawing and pottery.' Perhaps she had no particularly happy memories of school apart from the art classes.

Despite the fact that Phyllis was clearly a talented artist, winning prizes for drawing at school, her father would not let her to go to art school. At the time of the 1939 National Register, her occupation was given as 'tracer machine drawing'.

However, she retained her love of art, joining the Chesterfield Art Club when it was founded in 1929. Much of her work was a record of everyday life in Chesterfield in sketches and water colours. Rather different, was a picture of the Staveley tar works exhibited in 1935, which the *Derbyshire Times* said showed originality of choice and described it as 'a vigorous picture!'

In 1973, she 'proposed to make a series of drawings of the parts of Chesterfield which are to be altered or demolished'. This was in response to the plan to redevelop the town centre, which would have resulted in the demolition of the Market Hall and attractive buildings on Low Pavement, replacing them with a shopping mall (see Dame Jennifer Jenkins). By chance, she was in town on 12 February 1974, when she saw smoke billowing across New Square. On investigation, she found the Peacock public house on fire. She didn't see any flames, but said that 'it now looks like a tooth over-ready for extraction'. The fire revealed that it was a timber-framed building (now Peacock's coffee shop), an important factor in the rethink of the proposed development.

The fire at the Peacock

Phyllis was a well-known figure around the town. As well as being in business and an artist, she was Captain of Calow Girl Guides in the 1930s, and was a violinist with the Hasland Philharmonic String Orchestra. She had an allotment and, on a Saturday, she was often to be found on the popular Women's Institute market stall selling her produce. She died in August 1994. Chesterfield Museum and Art Gallery has a collection of her work.

Charlotte Harrison 1828-1868

Not all women had happy and successful lives. For some, in the days of rudimentary birth control and infant mortality, the story could be very different. Charlotte Drabble, aged 25, married John Harrison in April 1853. She was his second wife, the first having died the previous year, having had five children, only two of whom were still alive. Charlotte died in 1868, whilst giving birth to, or shortly after the birth of her 14th child (including two sets of twins) in just over 15 years of marriage. She had been pregnant for almost all her married life. In 1859, three of her children, together with Elizabeth Ann, one of the surviving children of John's first marriage (i.e. four children), died in just six weeks. Another child, born the same year, was given the name of Elizabeth Ann. In 1862, a second set of twins was born, who died aged four weeks and 12 weeks.

Five more children were born before Charlotte died, one of whom died at just three months old. An eight-year-old son died the following year. Charlotte herself died in 1868, aged 40, giving birth to, or shortly after the birth of Benjamin, who survived. Of her 14 children, six died aged three years and under.

The double slab tomb at Spital Cemetery

Marion died 1859 aged 3	*Charles died 1862 aged 5 weeks*
Elizabeth died 1859 aged 13	*Frederick died 1862 aged 12 weeks*
(Daughter of John's first wife)	*Alexander died 1865 aged 3 months*
Joseph died 1859 aged 2	*Charlotte 2nd wife died 1868 aged 40*
John died 1859 aged 2	

John married for a third time; his bride was Catherine Thompson Smith, who was 37. She inherited eight stepchildren between 23 and three years. The eldest was Catherine, a child of John's first marriage. Although Catherine junior was still with the family at the time of the 1871 census, the situation could have been difficult with two women called Catherine, with an age difference of 14 years, living in the same house. Nothing more is known of Catherine junior until John died in 1911, aged 93. His obituary stated that his eldest daughter (i.e. Catherine) was Mrs McGee, who was living in South Africa. She was one of the eight children surviving him, six others were Charlotte's (two having died after her death), and one from his third marriage.

John Harrison was well known in the town, having built up a boot and shoe business. Certainly, the family would not have been living in slum conditions. The business was taken over by two of his sons. In 1894, his third wife, Catherine, was elected a member of the Chesterfield Board of Guardians alongside Margaret Markham and Mary Swanwick. She died in 1900.

Rhoda Lucy Harrison 1892-1967

One of Charlotte's children who survived was Arthur Harrison. His eldest son, John Clifford Harrison, enlisted in the Sherwood Foresters on the outbreak of WWI. He was in the 9th Service Battalion when it sailed from Liverpool to Gallipoli in July 1915, arriving at Sula Bay in August, before being evacuated in December 1915. John was injured for the first time. The battalion was transferred to Egypt before embarking for France in July 1916, where it suffered major casualties during the Battle of the Somme. There were further major battles in 1917. By now a captain, John had been injured twice more. Presumably, he was now unfit for further combat, as he became Area Commandant attached to the 5th Army on the Northern Front in France. He was responsible for keeping the area clean and sanitary for troops not on duty in the line.

Rhoda Lucy Kelly was born in Montreal in 1892; she was two years older than John. In March 1917, she joined the Canadian Expeditionary Force in Toronto, becoming a staff nurse with the QAIMNSR, contracted to serve for one year.[3] Arriving in France in April 1917, Rhoda was sent to the number 4 General Hospital at Camiers, just north of Étaples, for ten months, before being sent to 5 Casualty Clearing Station at Tincourt, east of Peronne in the Somme area, for one month, and then to 41 Stationary Hospital at Amiens. It was probably at this time that she met John. Rhoda was as described as 'A very good nurse, very kind and attentive to her patients, much liked by them'. She sought to resign from the service at the end of her contract, giving her forthcoming marriage as the reason for her resignation. Nurses who married were required to leave the service. However, 21 March 1918 marked the beginning of the major German offensive, the brunt of which was born initially by the 5th Army, and arrangements for the wedding had to be postponed. Rather than sign another one year contract for QAIMNSR, Rhoda joined the Canadian Army Medical Corps, and was posted to 16 Canadian Hospital at Orpington, Kent, until she resigned on 17 June 1918, the day before John and Rhoda's military wedding at Chesterfield Parish Church. She wore the uniform of a First Lieutenant in the Canadian Army, which was the equivalent of a sister. They were possibly the best clothes that she had. Her brother was unable to get leave to attend, so she was given away her father-in-law to be. Officiating at the wedding was the Revd Henry Harrison of Radbourne, who was John's uncle, and Charlotte Harrison's eldest son.

3. https://livesofthefirstworldwar.iwm.org.uk/lifestory/5973421

At the time of the National Register in 1939, Rhoda was listed as a voluntary nursing sister at the Royal Hospital. In January 1940, she was appointed acting matron of a temporary hospital at Staveley set up for 19 patients, to treat soldiers who were billeted in the area, and who were suffering bronchial problems, due to the intense cold. A local chemist supplied several gallons of cough medicine free of charge! Later, she was a staff supervisor at Negretti and Zambra, when it was relocated to Chesterfield, John became commanding officer of the Chesterfield 331 squadron of air cadets.

Both were keen golfers. After the war, the couple moved to Ashover where Rhoda died in January 1967, and John the following September.

Hilda Hawes 1893-1974

Hilda Hawes was daughter of Arthur Hawes, a railway signalman, and his wife Betsy. They lived at Station Road, Whittington. In July 1915, after training, Hilda became a staff nurse at the Northern General Hospital in Sheffield. She became a member of the Territorial Forces Nursing Service and, volunteering for overseas service in March 1917, she was posted to Salonika in Greece. Sailing from Southampton to Le Havre, she travelled by train to Marseilles, where she boarded HMS *Transylvania*, together with a full complement of troops and 63 nurses. Escorted by two Japanese destroyers, the transport set sail for Alexandria. On 4 May, when the ship was approximately two miles south of Savona on the Gulf of Genoa, it was struck by a torpedo. Descriptions of what happened next vary. Hilda sent a letter home to her father, which was reprinted in the *Derbyshire Courier* of 5 June 1917. As one of the Japanese destroyers came alongside to take people off the ship, the *Transylvania* was hit by a second torpedo, and began to sink. According to Hilda, the boat that she was in became trapped in the wreckage, and they had to bail it out using their hats and shoes. They were in the water for about three hours, before they were rescued by one of the Japanese destroyers. All the nurses were saved, but ten crew members, 29 army officers and 373 soldiers were lost. The nurses were taken to a convent, where they were personally looked after by the nuns during the four days they were there. They were well treated by the townsfolk who found clothes for them, as they had lost practically everything.

H. M. S. Transylvania

The nurses returned to England for rest, recuperation, and to re-equip. Hilda complained that the £39 15s she received for replacing her uniform and equipment was inadequate, but was told that it was all she would get and what was a 'little loss of money when one's life had been saved'. This was all very well for the wealthy, but not for someone whose father was a railway signalman. On 14 June, she reported to the Northern General again. She was soon on her way to Salonika once more, where she joined the 48th General Hospital at Salonika, with its 1040 beds. Conditions in the Balkans were bad; more men died of disease than as the result of enemy action. The hospital specialised in treating dysentery and malaria. Several nurses contracted malaria, and in August 1918, Hilda succumbed. She returned to work, but another attack in October saw her evacuated to Malta for treatment, and then a spell in the Sisters Rest Home, before it was decided to send her back to England, where she arrived at Southampton on 13 December 1918. After medical boards' reports, she was declared fit for duty, but at the same time she was discharged from the service, as hospitals were being wound down. She found employment as a night sister at Eccles and Patricroft Hospital, a small hospital in Manchester. Hilda received a small allowance to remain on reserve, but, in 1923, she resigned, when she married Arthur Slack Green, an engine driver with the Midland Railway, back in Whittington. Arthur died in 1973, and Hilda a year later.

Betty Heathfield 1927-2006

Betty Vardy was the daughter of John William Vardy, a miner, and his wife Hannah, née Thompson. The couple had married the previous year; the birth of Betty was followed a year later by a sister, then a brother, followed by another sister in 1935. In 1939, the family was living with Hannah's mother Mary Ann Thompson in Shaw Street, Whittington Moor. At the time of her death, Mary Ann was said to have been living in the house for 56 years. When she first moved in, almost all the houses in the street were occupied by mining families. She had raised five sons and three daughters in a two-up two-down house. Her husband had been a miner, and Mary Ann, who had been born at Brampton in 1854, started work at Robinson & Sons at the age of nine years. She had a hard life.

Betty attended the newly-extended Cavendish Junior Girls' School, and at the age of 11 years, passed the scholarship examination to gain a place at Chesterfield Girls' High School. Although her results there in the School Certificate Examinations were good enough for her to stay on in the VIth form and perhaps try for a place at university, her family needed her to earn a wage. She left school in 1943 to become a secretary at a local engineering firm.

In December 1944, Harry Pollitt, the General Secretary of the Communist Party of Great Britain, visited Chesterfield to give a talk at the Cooperative Hall on Elder Way. It is likely that Betty attended this meeting and was encouraged to join the Young Communist League; she later became a member of Communist Party.

In 1953, Betty married Peter Heathfield at Chesterfield Register Office. Peter was born at Somercotes near Alfreton, but the family moved to Chesterfield where Peter went to school. Initially, he worked in a colliery drawing office, before he went underground at Williamthorpe Colliery from about 1947 until 1966, when he became a full-time union official with the National Union of Mineworkers. He became the Derbyshire Area Secretary in 1973, and the NUM general secretary in 1984, just five days before the miners' strike of 1984-5 began.

During the strike, following the example of Betty and the Derbyshire Women's Action Group, local women's groups were formed to support the striking miners. An umbrella group, Women Against Pit Closures, WAPC was established to help organise, sustain, and co-ordinate the local groups. Betty Heathfield and Anne Scargill were prominent in the campaign to raise money to help families of the miners by providing food, clothing, and holiday breaks for the schoolchildren. As the strike continued, women became more involved, joining marches, delivering speeches and joining the picket lines. Possibly, the support of the women helped prolong the strike. However, there were real tensions within the group, as it was controlled by an unelected committee, which was heavily influenced by the NUM leadership. Many NUM officials, both local and national, were wary of the involvement of women and the grassroots membership of WAPC were left feeling that they could have achieved more.

However, there can be no doubt about Betty's popularity with the miners' wives; she was one of them, and by her dedication and leadership, she attracted public support.

In 1989, the couple's marriage broke up, possibly due to strains brought about by the strike. They had three sons and a daughter.

Betty began studying for a politics degree at Lancaster University. Sadly, she fell ill with Alzheimer's disease; her last four years were spent in a Chesterfield nursing home where she died on 16 February 2006.

Dame Jennifer Jenkins 1921-2017

Mary Jennifer Jenkins was born in Chapel-en-le-Frith in 1921, the daughter of George Parker Morris (better known as Parker Morris) and his wife Dorothy Aylmer, née Hale. Like Olave Lady Baden-Powell and Barbara Castle, she made her name after she had left Chesterfield, and only a brief outline of her career is included here, but in the 1970s she played an important part in plans to redevelop the town centre.

Her father was Deputy Town Clerk of Salford, and the family moved to Chesterfield in 1923, when he became Town Clerk of Chesterfield, before becoming Town Clerk of Westminster at the beginning of 1929. He oversaw the incorporation of Whittington into the Borough of Chesterfield, and the demolition of slums in the town. Nationally, he is best known for the development of public housing standards in 1961. The popular family clearly had a happy time in Chesterfield, as her father returned to Chesterfield several times in the 1930s to spend time with his friends playing golf at Walton, and her mother attended meetings of the Chesterfield Women's Club.

Jennifer was educated at St Mary's School, Calne, Wiltshire before she went on to read history at Girton College. She married the Labour politician Roy Jenkins in 1947.

In 1962, a town plan was published which envisaged redevelopment of the central area, covering New Square, the Market Hall, and the Shambles and which involved building over the Market Square. Proposals included 80 shops and a five-storey office block, which could be extended to 11 storeys. In 1967, a revised town plan was presented to the Minister of Housing and Local Government, who ordered a public inquiry, which took three years to report. In 1972, the new development partners, Hammerson, put forward a smaller scheme proposing that the Market Place, Market Hall, and properties on Central Pavement should be demolished to make way for a shopping mall, including two pubs, 51 shops and parking for 660 cars. Opposition to the scheme was growing, but the council remained unmoved. The strength of the opposition was reported in the national press, and it was at this point that Jennifer Jenkins became involved. At the time, she was the secretary of the Ancient Monuments Society. She wrote a conciliatory letter to the Town Clerk 'offering to mediate between the council and the protesters'. His letter in reply was 'the curtest brush-off I have received in my life'.[4] She supported the campaign to save the Market Place; her advice and support must have been invaluable to the protestors. In February 1974, a fire damaged the Peacock public house (see Phyllis Hanson). Despite its importance, the Department of the Environment initially refused to list the building. In April 1974, Hammerson withdrew, but the arguments rumbled on, and it was not until mid-1975 that there was a proposal that the Department of the Environment (encouraged by Jennifer Jenkins) should get together with the council, to jointly appoint and pay for consultants to investigate whether a conservation approach was feasible for the proposed development. As result, the council was persuaded to try a conservation-orientated approach. The result was 'an outstanding example of urban renewal in the United Kingdom.'

Jennifer was the chairman of the Historic Buildings Commission from 1975 until 1984. She helped to organise the recording of parks and gardens for the *Register of Historic Parks and Gardens*, published in 1984 in which Queen's Park was listed as Grade I, more recently upgraded to Grade I*.

Jennifer was created a Dame of the British Empire in 1985. She died in February 2017.

Sarah Johnson 1761-1831

Sarah Johnson was baptised at Norbury near Ashbourne the daughter of William Johnson and his wife Margaret, née Wright. Margaret had two brothers, Samuel and William, a sister Sarah, and a second sister Elizabeth, who married John Deakin, landlord of the Falcon Inn on Low Pavement, Chesterfield.

4. Aldous, Terry New Shopping in Historic Towns. English Heritage. 1990 p 18.

Sarah had two brothers, also called Samuel and William, and a sister Margaret, who married Thomas Greaves. Sarah went to live with her aunt Elizabeth at the Falcon Inn. Her uncle, John Deakin, died in 1812. In his will he left his property to his wife Elizabeth and, on her death, to Elizabeth's sister, Sarah (Wright), and Sarah Johnson, daughter of Elizabeth's sister Margaret, and lastly to his brother-in-law John Wright.

The *Derby Mercury* of 27 March 1817 carried the following notice:

ANGEL INN AND POST HOUSE, CHESTERFIELD. SARAH JOHNSON most respectfully informs the Public, that she has entered into the above Inn, lately occupied by Mr. Peech, which is new fitted up in a very superior manner. S. J. avails herself of this Opportunity to thank her numerous friends conferred upon her during the many years she resided at the Falcon and begs to assure them that no attention or exertion shall be wanting to render the Angel Inn worthy of their Patronage and Support.

P. S. An extensive and choice Stock of Old Wines constantly at hand.

The Angel was an inn on the High Street, opposite where the Market Hall now stands. It played a prominent part in the commercial and social life of Chesterfield, until it was destroyed by fire in February 1917.

It was described as having several parlours; a coffee room; a dining room, used also as an assembly room; and a great number of lodging rooms. The yard, which extended to Saltergate, contained a barn, stables, hay-chambers, corn chambers, coach-houses and a garden.

In April 1819, a meeting of local landowners and farmers at

the Angel Inn resulted in the formation of the Scarsdale & High Peak Agricultural Society. The first agricultural show was held later that year. From these humble beginnings evolved the Derbyshire Agricultural Society and the Bakewell Show. Sarah became a member of the society. Also in 1819, Sarah's mother died.

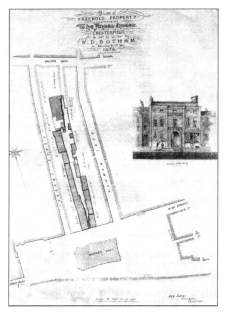

Plan of the Angel at the time of its sale, in 1876

Frequently, bankruptcy hearings were heard at the Angel, and there were meetings for the letting of toll gates. The Chesterfield Association for the Prosecution of Felons met there. Membership was available to anyone who lived within four miles of Chesterfield on the payment of an annual sum. Sarah was one of only seven female members out of a total membership of over 100. Property sales were held at the Angel, and catalogues could be consulted for sales in different parts of the country. One of the most important sales locally was in 1824, when properties in the Chesterfield area were sold after the death of the Marquis of Ormonde. Sarah purchased Somersall Hall, the adjoining farm and a seat in Brampton (Old Brampton) Church for £11,700 gns. She must have been quite a wealthy woman, but she still had to take out a mortgage.

The notice of her death appeared in *Derby Mercury* for 23 December 1831:

'On Saturday, the 17th instant. Miss Sarah Johnson, aged 70 years. She for many years most respectably filled the situation of Innkeeper and post-mistress at the Falcon and Angel Inns, Chesterfield. Her death will be long and deservedly lamented by her relatives, and also by many who benefitted by her numerous charities, both in public and in private life. It was her intention to retire from business, to reside upon some property she had at Somersall in the parish of Brampton, and Saturday was fixed for her removal, but death defeated her purpose. Her remains were conveyed on Thursday last, for internment, to Norbury near Ashbourne'.

Her personal estate was valued at £1,500. She left the property at Somersall to her brother Samuel, subject to the payment of the debts on the mortgage. The rest of her property she left to her brothers, Samuel and William, and her sister, Margaret Greaves, in equal shares and proportions as tenants in common not as joint tenants. In 1849, at the time of the tithe valuation, Thomas Greaves, husband of Margaret, owned the Angel Inn and Samuel owned several small plots in the town. William owned no property in the town – his share was probably elsewhere.

Sarah Johnson was unusual in being a property owner in the town and running her own business. Most other women running businesses were widows continuing to run the business after the death of their husbands. Unfortunately for Sarah, she was running the Angel at a time when Sir Richard Phillips, in his book of travels entitled *A Picture of England*, regarded Chesterfield as a dull, worn-out town, where the residents were dull and lacking in ambition for change. This changed with the opening of the railway in 1840, and the Angel, with its extensive coaching facilities was ideally placed to serve travellers using the railway.

Winifred 1876-1955 and Gladys Jones 1878-1953

Winifred and Gladys were the daughters of William Tom Jones, a solicitor and a partner of John Middleton (the Town Clerk), in the practice of Jones and Middleton. William married Dorothy Sarah Robinson, daughter of Thomas Robinson, the Secretary of the Staveley Coal and Iron Company. They lived at Cross Street, Chesterfield, where Winifred was born in January 1876. Her sister Gladys was born in 1878, by which time the family was living at Spital Lodge.

In 1902, Winifred attended a meeting of the Chesterfield Women's Liberal Association to hear a talk on '*Municipal Trading and Liberal Principles*'. In 1907, she attended a meeting of the Chesterfield Civic Guild, which had been established earlier in the year, for the purpose of relieving the poor in the days before state support became more readily available.

Winifred first came to public notice in October 1909, when she threw a stone through a window of the Palace Theatre, Newcastle, on the occasion of a visit by David Lloyd George. Lady Lytton, who was charged with doing £4 damage to a car (her second offence), was bound over. Mrs Brailsford, who struck a barrier with an axe, was bound over and released after two-and-a-half days. Winifred (a first offender) was charged with doing £1 damage to a window, and was sentenced to 14 days hard labour. The women were committed to Newcastle jail, where they went on hunger strike. Lady Lytton was discharged after two days, the reason given being that she had a weak heart. This annoyed Lady Lytton, who wrote a letter to *The Times* complaining that she and Mrs Brailsford had been released, whereas Winifred had been jailed for a first offence and a lesser crime.

In June 1910, the militant Women's Socialist and Political Union held a meeting in the Market Hall Assembly Rooms. Winifred handed out leaflets and collected donations. The principal speaker at the meeting was Adele Pankhurst. There was not a great deal of support for the suffragettes in Chesterfield; the support was rather for the non-militant suffragists – the National Union of Women's Suffrage Societies.

Winifred addressing an audience in the Market Place
accompanied by her sister Gladys

On 18 November 1910, there were violent scenes outside the Houses of Parliament, when Prime Minister Asquith refused to allow time to consider the Parliamentary Franchise (Women's)

Bill. Winifred and Jessie Smith were among the 117 people arrested, but were released without charge. A few days later, Winifred was arrested and charged with wilful damage of 10 Downing Street, for which she was fined £5 3s 6d or one month in jail. Usually suffragettes faced with paying a fine or going to jail, chose to go to jail. However, her father was unwell and she may have paid her fine instead. William Jones died in January 1911, and Winifred attended his funeral. She is missing from the 1911 census; like many other suffragettes and suffragists, she may have refused to fill in the form.

What happened to Winifred after that is not known. However, she was at Eagle House at Batheaston, a home of refuge for suffragettes, when she planted a tree on 2 July 1911, suggesting that she might have been involved in another suffragette action in the meantime. This is the last we hear of Winifred's suffragette activities.[5]

Although Gladys had accompanied her sister to the meeting of the Civic Guild, she did not become a suffragette. She began publishing under the pen name, Gwen John. In 1912, the *Derbyshire Courier* carried an article with the headline 'Chesterfield Lady's Banned Play' about *Edge o' Dark,* which had been banned by the Lord Chamberlain. The author was identified as Gwen John, the pen name of a Chesterfield suffragist. The *Derbyshire Courier* was somewhat critical of the play, referring to it as the sort of case 'we hear of now and then in our police courts in which the 'lodger' looms large', and 'She makes her characters speak in this sketch as the magistrates only allow them to speak behind closed doors'. The following week Winifred wrote to the *Derbyshire Courier* in support of her sister saying that 'women in their comfortable drawing rooms with good husbands and good friends ought not to be kept in ignorance' and that all women ought to have compassion for

5. There are other references to a Winifred Jones but she was from Middlesbrough and is a different person.

their less fortunate sisters, who were alone and unprotected in sordid surroundings.

Gladys moved to London, where she joined the Pioneer Players, a society which initially produced plays intended to promote women's suffrage and feminism, but later a series of plays by writers such as Checkhov were performed. As a private subscription society, it was able to produce plays which might otherwise have been banned by the Lord Chamberlain. Under her pen name, Gwen John, she wrote books, plays and poems, and she also produced plays, appeared on the London stage and eventually on the wireless. Probably her best known play was *Luck of War*, produced in 1917, in which a young woman is left behind with two young children, when her husband goes off to war at the first opportunity. Her husband is presumed dead after the battle at Neuve Chapelle. She takes in a lodger and, when another child is on its way, the couple marry. Her first husband reappears having been in hospital after losing a foot. Some people felt that she had married too quickly, but the author blamed the workings of the separation allowance and the pension system, which had left a young woman on her own and facing poverty.

Gladys returned to Chesterfield in 1914, when she presented a paper at the opening of an exhibition of the work of the artist, Joseph Syddall. She was described as being 'well known in the literary world'.

The Representation of the People Act 1918 abolished practically all property qualifications for men over 21, and enfranchised women over 30 who met minimum property qualifications. Now Gladys turned to historical themes. In December 1925, *Gloriana* (about Elizabeth I) was produced at the Little Theatre, with eight acts and 70 characters (including John Gielgud). The play received a mixed reception, and then Gladys wrote a biography of Queen Elizabeth, which received a favourable review from the *Derbyshire Times*.

In 1928, a brief news item in *The Times* reported the unveiling of a statue of Queen Elizabeth in a niche above the vestry door of St Dunstan's in the West on Fleet Street, by Dame Millicent Fawcett and mentioning the assistance given by Gwen John and Miss Jones. Given the link with Millicent Fawcett, and Mrs Pethick Lawrence (later Lady Pethick Lawrence), it is possible that Winifred changed from a militant suffragette to one who used non-violent methods of protest.

The two sisters had a flat in Lincoln's Inn Fields and a country cottage near Burford, Oxfordshire. In the National Register of 1939, Winifred and her sister (enumerated as Gwen John) were living in the small village of Asthall on the banks of the Windrush in Oxfordshire. Winifred and Gladys remained at Asthall until their deaths, but they were buried in the family vault in Old Brampton churchyard. Gladys died on 3 May 1953 and Winifred on 30 October 1955. She left £44,000, including £2,000 to the RSPCA, subject to the society taking charge of her pets or animals and placing them in country homes. After the rest of her bequests, the residue was left to the Distressed Gentlefolks' Aid Association.

Annie King 1870-1900

Sarah Annie King (also known as Annie) was born at Charlton Kings in Gloucestershire in 1870, the seventh child of Thomas King, a butcher, and his wife Susannah. In 1891, she was recorded as being her mother's helper. There is no obvious reason why she should be in Chesterfield in May 1893 when she was elected a teacher at the Ragged School. Her elder brother Ernest was living in Masbrough (Rotherham), where he was a clerk for a corn miller. Perhaps, he had visited the corn mills in Chesterfield or had contact with the Ragged School. Chesterfield was connected with Masbrough on a direct rail line. Annie found employment as a draper's assistant at Messrs Taylor Bros. Fancy and General Drapers (where Clarke's shoe shop now is).

Annie arrived at a bad time for Chesterfield. Leading up to 1893 too much coal was being extracted, as a result of which there was an over-supply. The price of coal fell. In June of that year, out of an estimated 15,000 miners in the district, 9,000 were on two days' work a week, and the remainder out of work altogether. By the end of July a dispute between the Coal-Owners' Association (who wanted a 25% cut in miners' wages) and the miners, resulted in a lock-out, which continued until November, when the men went back to work at their original wage. The economic effect on a town, which depended so much on the mines and the industries which supported them for employment was harsh, and inevitably the poorer sections of the community suffered most. In the middle of October, T. P. O'Connor MP visited Chesterfield. He was touring the most distressed areas in England, and found parts of Chesterfield the worst. He was the owner/editor of the *Sun* evening paper in London, and an article published there resulted in a considerable sum of money being donated by readers to alleviate the distress in Chesterfield.

Some of the worst conditions were to be found in the narrow, overcrowded, and insanitary yards surrounding the Ragged School. Annie was soon very involved in the Sunday school, which was held both in the morning and evening. She was a participant in teacher's meetings and a member of the committee running the Ragged School.

Despite local hardships, the Ragged School managed to make donations to missions overseas. Annie was moved by the stories she heard, and in 1898, she resolved to join the China Inland Mission. On 14 August, she took a major part in the morning, afternoon and evening services, before leaving to join the mission. She left behind many friends, who were sorry to see her go. The China Inland Mission sought to bring Christianity to the Chinese, and also to help them overcome opium addiction. On reaching China, all new missionaries had to attend special training colleges to learn the language and customs, before they were sent to a location, where they could improve their language skills and begin evangelistic work under the supervision of more experienced missionaries. All had to wear Chinese dress. A letter was received from her a year later, when she had reached her destination and started work. Possibly, this was at Ho-tsin in Shansi Province (now Hejin in Shanxi Province in Northern China to the west of Bejing), where George and Bella McConnell were stationed. In the summer of 1900, she went with the McConnells and another young missionary, Elizabeth Burton, to spend the summer in the hills near San Heo. They were enjoying a pleasant peaceful holiday, until news arrived about Boxer violence in the province. The Boxer rebellion, an anti-foreigner uprising by the Militia in Righteousness (nicknamed the Boxers), took place between 1899 and 1901. Major causes of discontent in north China were that foreign missionaries had the freedom to preach anywhere in China, and to buy land on which to build churches.

The party decided to return to Ho-tsin. They were joined by two fellow missionaries, John Young from Scotland, and his American wife Alice (née Troyer) from Indiana. Then, the group heard about disturbances and disorder in Ho-tsin, with reports of maltreatment and persecution of foreigners by the Boxers. So they headed south instead, towards the Yellow River. A band of mounted soldiers overtook them, saying that they had been sent by the provincial governor to escort them to safety. The soldiers advised them to take a quiet road to a place called Ts'ing-kia-uan, where a ferry boat would be provided for them. However, when the group arrived they realised they had been deceived. The soldiers then revealed that they were Boxers. They told the missionaries that, unless they stopped worshipping God and preaching against idolatry, they would kill them. The missionaries refused, and the party of six missionaries, the child of the McConnells and a native servant were brutally murdered.[6] Altogether, 58 missionaries of the CIM and 21 of their children lost their lives during the Boxer rebellion.

Her death was received with great sadness in Chesterfield, but the chapel register simply records:

'August 2nd 1900. News received that Miss King has been murdered'.

A memorial tablet was commissioned from a local mason, Mr Hollis, a member of the chapel. Her brother Ernest came from Masbrough to take the evening service on 6 October 1900. Her death is recorded in Consular Deaths at Shanghai as S. King.

Annie's memorial at the Ragged School

6. https://www.evangelical-times.org/20363/the-noble-army-of-martyrs/

Susan Mallinson 1942-2016

Susan Colledge was born in Chesterfield, the daughter of Sydney Colledge, manager of Roy Smith's electrical store, and his wife Molly née Francis. As well as studying for her qualification from the Guildhall School Music and Drama, Molly frequently gave recitations at fund raising events. By 1943, she was offering coaching for the elementary examinations of the Guildhall School of Music and Drama, so it's not surprising that Susan joined the classes. She was educated at Highfield Hall School and St Helena (formerly the Girls' High School). Whilst at St Helena, she was on the committee of the Junior Dramatic Society. At the Senior School Speech Day in 1958, she was the contralto soloist when the choir performed part of *Hadyn's Creation*.

This was during Susan's last year at school. At the age of 16 years, Susan was the youngest person to be admitted (at that time) to the Guildhall School of Music and Drama. For the first year, she did not get a grant from Derbyshire County Council, as the headmistress of St Helena at the time thought that she would benefit from more time at school. Although she entered Guildhall as a singer, she also studied the four-year speech and drama course.

After completing the course, during which she was awarded the Guildhall's contralto prize, she went on to complete her Speech and Drama Teacher's Diploma. Unfortunately, she was unsuccessful in her applications for parts in musicals, but she was successful in gaining the post of English teacher in a kindergarten in Barcelona. Whilst in Spain, she was fortunate enough to be able to study under Conchita Badia, the leading singer and teacher in Spain. She was helped by a grant from the Spanish Government to study the interpretation of Spanish folk music. She also performed in concerts as an opera singer around Spain.

Susan returned to England four years later, but was still unsuccessful in getting work in the theatre. Once more, she took a teaching post – this time at a school in Kensington, eventually becoming assistant head.

In 1972, she married Stuart Mallinson, and the couple lived at Kingston upon Thames before moving to Huddersfield, Stuart's home town. Unfortunately, the marriage was not a happy one and Susan divorced her husband. In 1980, she was living in Holmfirth. She was fortunate enough to receive a gift from a relative which enabled her to rent a flat over a shop in Holmfirth, which she turned into the Speech Studio in 1994. She taught the art of public speaking to a wide range of people, from footballers to judges, and news presenters to clergy. She also taught elocution in local private schools.

Last of the Summer Wine was being filled in Holmfirth at the time and, as she was a member of Equity, she was able to appear as a barmaid in two episodes. Following another gift from a relative she was able to go cruising with a friend. Having listened to good, bad and indifferent speakers and, aware that she had led an interesting life, she applied to P & O and Fred Olsen for the position of guest speaker, and was successful.

Something she did not expect was the opportunity to appear in two films in Spain. In 2004, she was a matron in a hostel for down and outs in a psychological thriller; in 2006, she appeared as Colonel Frankenheimer in a musical comedy.

Susan returned to Chesterfield in 2009, when she continued to give classes in elocution. She died in 2016.

Further information may be found in the *Derbyshire Life and Countryside* October 2011.

Margaret Markham 1864-1936

Margaret Hermine Jackson (also known as Daisy) was the daughter of Thomas Hughes Jackson and his wife Hermine née Meinertzhagen. She had two sisters and eight brothers. In her early days, she was keen on sport and outdoor recreation. The family lived at Claughton Manor House, overlooking Birkenhead Park (since demolished), and in 1917, her father was Mayor of Birkenhead. Her grandfather was Sir William Hughes Jackson, originally a partner, and later the sole proprietor of Clay Cross Coal and Iron Works. The company would remain in the hands of the Jackson family. It is probably through this connection that she met Charles Markham. The couple married at Birkenhead Parish Church on 6 June 1889. The couple made their home briefly at Spring Bank House on Ashgate Road, before moving to Hasland Hall in August 1891, and then to Ringwood Hall in 1911 or 1912.

With her background, it is not surprising that Margaret soon became involved in the public and social activities in the area. In 1894, she was elected to the Board of Guardians to represent Hasland. She took a particular interest in the Children's Home at Ashgate and, together with Mrs Edmunds, provided the children with a Christmas treat, and laid on a summer excursion for the old people in the Workhouse. She was president of Magdalen House, which provided support for unmarried mothers, young girls and teenagers, who had no family to support them. She was connected with the Chesterfield and North Derbyshire Hospital (later the Royal Hospital) from 1900, becoming a member of the Board of Management. She was concerned with the welfare of inmates of the County Mental Institution and a member of the County Nursing Association. Her experience led to her being one of the first co-opted members of Derbyshire County Council. She was appointed a borough magistrate in 1920 and county magistrate in 1921. She was the first Divisional Commissioner of Chesterfield Girl Guides and a supporter of the British Legion. When Charles Markham was Mayor of Chesterfield in 1896, 1909 and 1910, she was his mayoress. As her obituary said 'In the course of her life she must have opened some hundreds of church bazaars and similar functions.'

Unfortunately, their marriage was a stormy one, which ended in divorce in 1925. Margaret left Ringwood Hall to live at South Wingfield Manor. She said: "I will grieve to leave Ringwood Hall especially the garden." When opening an exhibition of the Chesterfield and District Smallholders' Association, she said: "I think that if I had to choose a way of livelihood, it would be gardening." The gardens at Hasland Hall and Ringwood Hall were frequently opened to the public to raise funds for good causes.

Living at South Wingfield Hall, she continued her public duties, until she had to retire through ill health some months before her death on 9 October 1936 at the age of 72.

Her obituary in the *Derbyshire Times* was headed 'A Life of Public Service' - the same words which headed the obituary of Mary Swanwick, yet she has been largely forgotten in Chesterfield compared with her contemporaries Blanche Eastwood, Violet Markham and Mary Swanwick. Like the wives of other prominent men in the town, her work was overshadowed by that of her husband.

Violet Markham 1872-1959

Violet Rosa Markham was born at Brimington Hall (now demolished) in 1872, the daughter of Charles Markham and his wife Rosa, the daughter of Sir Joseph Paxton. She had three brothers Ernest, who died aged 21, Charles Paxton, and Arthur Basil. The family moved to Tapton House in 1873. She had a happy childhood. A family gathering always included discussions about public affairs, particularly politics, including the Boer War and later Home Rule for Ireland. She was taught at home, but in retrospect, felt that her education had serious blanks as she was not taught the Bible, Shakespeare, German and arithmetic. Although she was fluent in French from an early age, thanks to her mother's French maid and a French governess, in later life she struggled to learn German, but arithmetic was a lifelong stumbling block. She was later sent to school at West Heath, a small school near Richmond, Surrey, where training concentrated on social airs and graces. The girls were not taught science, economics or social history, although they did have lecturers from London. However, she was always grateful for the lessons in elocution, which helped with her public speaking in later life. She was at the school for eighteen months.

In 1898, at the age of 26 years, she was elected to the Chesterfield School Board, which involved frequent visits to the schools. The board was ahead of its time in attempting to raise the standard of children's education by raising the standard that the children had to reach before they could leave school. This reduced the pool of cheap, child labour and prevented parents increasing the family's income by sending young children out to work. This was unpopular with some people, and along with some of the other members, she lost her seat on the board after the election of 1901.

School boards were abolished in 1902, as local authorities took over responsibility for elementary education. As Violet was not on the council, she was not on the Education Committee, but was co-opted onto the Committee in 1903.

In 1901, she received an unexpected legacy, which enabled her to buy a house in London, at 8 Gower Street, where she was able to entertain important people in the social services and political communities. At the time of the 1911 census, Florence Robinson and Jessie Smith from Chesterfield were staying there. Violet Markham was entered as 'a boarding house keeper', although she was at Tapton at the time; she was, therefore, enumerated in two places.

In April 1907, the Chesterfield Civic Guild was formed, with the object of deepening the sense of responsibility for the care of the poor, and to create a neighbourly feeling amongst all classes of the community. Violet was on the executive committee. It was wound up in 1920, because of shortage of funds and the extension of state provision. The work was then taken over by a newly-formed Borough Welfare Committee composed of members of the council, the Board of Guardians, and representatives of voluntary bodies. Immediately, 13 members were co-opted, including nine women, one of whom was Violet Markham. Eventually, it was extended to include representatives of every charity and philanthropic society in the town.

Of her brothers, Violet was closest to Arthur, sharing his concerns for the social welfare of his workers. She was very involved when he commissioned the construction of Woodlands, the colliery village for Brodsworth Main Colliery near Doncaster, on garden city lines. The buildings included pithead baths, a community centre, and a shop run by Doncaster Co-operative Society. Unfortunately, the local press gave the credit for the innovative scheme to Arthur's mother, saying she 'took a keen interest in the welfare of working people and their general social improvement. She perceived that this could be best begun by, first of all, placing them under higher domestic conditions'.

Somewhat surprisingly for one so far ahead of her time in matters of social welfare and education, Violet was anti-suffrage in her views before WWI. She felt that women lacked the education necessary to engage in political debate, and that they should be concerned with the welfare of their families. However, it was soon apparent during the war that there was a need for an army of working women and Violet modified her views.

During the war, she had been on committees dealing with the National Relief Fund and all aspects of the employment of women, including the welfare of munitions workers. In 1918, she spent eight days in France, some of them close enough to the front line to feel the atmosphere of battle. She did this as part of the commission set up to investigate slanderous accusations made against the women of the Women's Army Auxiliary Corps (see Minnie Wheatcroft). Few signs of immoral conduct were found in a company of 6,000 women. The only person who could have been accused of loose behaviour was the Honorary Secretary of the commission, Violet Markham, who was found entertaining a man in her bedroom. In 1915, she married James Carruthers, but kept her private and public lives quite separate. Consequently, to the public, it was Miss Markham who was entertaining a man, rather than Lt. Col. Carruthers, who was spending a short time with his wife. In recognition of her services during the war, Violet was one of the first four women created a Companion of Honour in June 1917. In 1942, she was appointed chairwoman of a committee of enquiry into the amenities and conditions of women's war service.

Arthur was Liberal MP for Mansfield from 1900 until his sudden death in 1916. At the 1918 General Election, Violet stood there as a Liberal candidate. Despite the enfranchisement of women over 30 who met minimum property qualifications, and her appeal to women, she only came third, as Labour took the seat for the first time.

Violet spent two years after the ending of the war in Germany, where her husband was part of the Army of Occupation, but by 1923, she was again co-opted onto the Education Committee, the chairman of which was Harry Cropper.

Between the wars, Violet was chairman of the Central Committee on Women's Training and Employment.

In 1925, Violet stood as a Liberal candidate in a municipal by-election in Trinity Ward, Chesterfield, in place of Mr Mansell, the former headmaster of the Grammar School, who had moved away after his retirement. She was returned by a large majority. The first woman councillor; she was joined later in the year by Blanche Eastwood.

Voilet Markham, Vice Chairman of the Education Committee

A highlight of Violet's year as Mayor (1927/8) was the opening of the girls' school on Highfield Lane, which bore her name, at the beginning of the reorganisation of education in the borough. As Mayor of Chesterfield, she received an invitation to the Cutlers' Feast in Sheffield. Unfortunately, women were not allowed to attend the Feast, so a compromise was reached; Violet was to be served dinner in a separate room and to listen to the speeches from a balcony. She declined the invitation!

To mark her year of office, she presented a pendant showing a Tudor rose, to be added to the Mayoral chain. She also presented the silver-gilt collarette, now used as the Mayoress's chain.

In 1927, a woman Housing Manager was appointed to work with tenants, in particular, those who had been rehoused on the St Augustine's estate. Chesterfield was the first authority outside London to make such an appointment. Janet Mary Upcott was another remarkable lady. She had trained in housing management at the London School of Economics, and worked under Octavia Hill, one of the founders of the National Trust. Janet spent 56 years on the Estates Committee of the Trust. During WWI, she had been in Serbia with the Scottish Women's Hospital. She was also a founder of the Association of Women Housing Managers. Although she didn't stay long, she was said to have made a significant difference to the estates, before moving on to a greater challenge at Stockton-on-Tees, as other local authorities followed Chesterfield's example.

In 1931, Violet resigned from the council and, in 1934, she resigned from the Education Committee because of the pressure of work. She had been the only woman to be appointed to the Unemployment Assistance Board. She also turned down the award of Honorary Freeman of the Borough of Chesterfield.

However, she had time to write *Paxton and Bachelor Duke*, the story of her grandfather and the Duke of Devonshire.

At the age of 76, Violet went to Saltergate to watch Chesterfield FC lose to Cardiff City 0-1, because she thought she ought to see a game. At half-time, when she was being entertained to tea, she remarked that it had been interesting. It wasn't the first time she had been to Saltergate. In 1927, she kicked off a match between members of the Town Council and Borough Officials, again she was supporting the losing side.

In December 1902, Violet financed the opening of the Chesterfield Settlement, in a building at the corner of Church Lane and Packers Row. Initially, the object was to provide pleasant social evenings for the working girls of the town, with amusements, a library and sewing classes. It was open three evenings a week for girls over 16 years of age, and two evenings for girls under that age. The subscription was 1d a week for seniors and ½d for juniors.

Violet and the newly-appointed warden, Elsie Willis, went round the works of Robinson & Sons and some of the potteries, dropping leaflets about the new girls' club and inviting members. As a result, between 80 and 100 girls attended the first meeting. Over the years, it was extended to include a Mother's Club, a Young Married Club, and a School for Mothers designed to provide an education in baby care and domestic hygiene. At one time, it was so popular that an offshoot, Everybody's Club, was formed at Brampton to reduce the pressure on accommodation. Classes for the mentally-and physically-handicapped were introduced. The organisation went from strength to strength. At its height, there were 13 social and recreational clubs and six educational classes attached to it. In 1942, there was a celebration of the fortieth anniversary of the club, and there were great plans for the future. Violet had funded the organisation from the start, but now the finances were put on a firmer footing. Sadly, the Settlement was wound up in 1957. Its reason for existence, education and welfare provision, had been taken over by government measures. A closing service was held at the Parish Church, when Violet Markham 'read' the lesson which she memorised because of failing eyesight.

The Settlement had always been a great joy to Violet, but she acknowledged that it had grown up through the work done by the efforts of other people. She regarded the whole as a string of pearls, with Violet herself being the string and the workers the pearls.

At the service, Florence Robinson said that Violet Markham was years ahead of her time in her desire for social reform.

In 1952, she became an Honorary Freeman of the Borough of Chesterfield, the honour she had turned down in 1935. Violet Markham died at her home in Kent on 2 February 1959.

More about her public service away from Chesterfield can be found in her autobiography *Return Passage* and *Friendship's Harvest*.

Emma Miller 1839-1917

Emma Holmes was born on 26 June 1839, the daughter of Daniel Holmes, a boot and shoe maker, and his wife Martha, née Hollingworth. They were married at St Peter and Paul, Sheffield (now the Cathedral), in 1838. By the time Emma was born, they were living in Parker's Yard off Holywell Street, with Daniel's father Samuel, a stocking frame worker.

Jonas Chapman's map of Chesterfield 1837

At the time, Chesterfield was very different from the town of today. It consisted of a small built-up area, which was surrounded by green fields.

However, it was entering a period of great change. The North Midland Railway opened in 1840, unlocking London as a market for coal. With improvements in technology, deep shafts allowed the mines to be sunk to the east of the town, rather than the shallow mines to the west. The population of the town increased rapidly; between 1851 and 1871 it almost doubled. The jobs which were created, particularly for miners and labourers, were low paid, and families moving into the town could only afford to live in the narrow yards, which rapidly degenerated into slums. Craft jobs like lace making and stocking-frame working were disappearing. Daniel's father had been a framework knitter.

By 1851, the family was living in Saltergate, and Emma had two sisters, Ann and Mary Elizabeth, and a brother, Ernest

Charles. Daniel was a member of Elder Yard Chapel, where Emma was able to learn to read and write at the Sunday school there.

Having lived in Sheffield where the Chartists were very active, Daniel was a keen supporter of the movement which sought equal rights for all men of whatever class, but there was little support for them in Chesterfield, possibly because the Duke of Devonshire owned much of the property. In April 1839, a march began in Sheffield, continued to Chesterfield, and then to Brampton Moor, where the meeting was addressed by speakers from Sheffield. Few people from Chesterfield joined the march, but the crowd was eventually reported to be 2000 at Brampton. A radical association had been formed in Brampton, and a meeting was held, at which a combined Brampton and Chesterfield United Radical Association was formed. Fifty women joined a women's association to support the men. Apart from a meeting in Ashover of stocking-frame workers, nothing more is heard of Chartist meetings in the area. Emma remembered walking with her father up to ten or 12 miles to meetings. These were most likely to be in Sheffield.

Jabez Silcock was born in Brampton, the son of George Silcock and his wife Hannah, in 1832. In 1851, he was working as a clerk in a shipping office in Manchester, but four years later he was back in Chesterfield, where he faced a court martial by the Chatsworth Rifles for drunkenness; he was reduced in rank from corporal to private. On 15 September 1857, Emma married Jabez at Chesterfield Registry Office. A son Thomas was born three months later. At the time of the 1861 census, the couple were living in Bank Yard, off Low Pavement. Emma was still working for her father and Jabez was a bookkeeper. A daughter, Mary Elizabeth, was born there.

About the same time, work started on New Road in

Brampton (now known as Chatsworth Road), where John Silcock kept a beerhouse. Possibly, he was a relative, and Jabez and Emma took it over, as a second daughter Catherine was born at New Road in 1865. Jabez was keeping a beerhouse there in June 1866, when he was charged with keeping his house open at unlawful hours. Emma appeared in court on Jabez's behalf, saying that her husband was unable to attend because of an attack of rheumatism. The beerhouse should have closed at 11pm the previous evening, but when PC O'Connor entered the house at 12:15 the next day, he found Jabez and two men, who had apparently been gambling, and there was a jug of beer on the table. Emma claimed they were doing nothing wrong, as one man was a lodger and the other a neighbour. The inference was that they were friends rather than customers – if they had been doing something wrong they might have fastened the back door. Emma asked PC O'Connor if he had any cause to complain of the way in which they had conducted the house up to that time. Unfortunately for her, he answered "yes", which caused much laughter. Perhaps the magistrate, Mr Lucas, felt some sympathy as they were only fined £1 and costs, which was paid promptly, but they were warned that any future appearance in court would be treated more severely.

Emma was probably a stronger character than her husband; it may have been her idea to move to Manchester, away from the temptations of the beerhouse and the atmospheric pollution caused by the potteries of Brampton, and in the hope that Jabez could once more get a job as a clerk. Instead, it was probably the worst period in Emma's life.

Although increasingly there were problems of poor housing and insanitary conditions in Chesterfield, these were magnified in Manchester, where the vast mill buildings continually emitted smoke, shut out air and light from the workers' dwellings, and filled the air with noise.

A fourth child, George, was born in Manchester, before the family moved to Salford. About the same time, her father lost his home in Saltergate, because he failed to pay his rent, and his goods were sold to pay the arrears. Daniel moved to Brampton in June 1866, possibly to the Silcock's house. In December 1866, he tried to hang himself after he had been drinking. Fortunately, a neighbour managed to cut him down before it was too late. The following July, he was in court for failing to pay gas and water bills dating back to June 1865.

Jabez died at the age of 38 on 1 June 1870. Emma was able to afford a respectable funeral with coaches and black-plumed horses. In 1871, Emma's parents were living with her, but were entered in the census as Daniel and Mary Hickman. Had they left Chesterfield without paying their bills? With four children to support, Emma became a seamstress, working 12 hours a day for six days a week. She remarried in 1874. Her new husband was William Calderwood, a widower and stone mason. Unfortunately, his lungs were seriously affected by the dust from his work and he developed phthisis, a type of tuberculosis. At the time, the newspapers carried advertisements offering free passages to Australia for domestic servants and farm labourers. In November 1878, William and Emma set sail on the barque *Selkirk* on an assisted passage with George, Mary, and Kate. Thomas stayed behind, but followed a year later. The family settled in Brisbane, but unfortunately, William died in 1880, and Emma was again having to provide for the family.

She became a gentleman's cotton shirt maker. She married for a third time in 1886. Her husband was Andrew Miller, a widower and Customs House agent. Her personal circumstances improved and she became more politically active. Four years later, Emma helped found Brisbane's first Women's Union, which campaigned against the no-sitting rule, which forced teachers and shop assistants to remain standing during their working day of 12 hours. In 1891, she gave evidence to the Royal Commission into Shops, Factories and Workshops. Emma championed equal pay and equal opportunity for women, and was foundation president of the Woman's Equal Franchise Association (1894-1905). She was widowed again in 1897. Emma was a founding member of the Workers' Political Organisation in Brisbane, a forerunner of the Australian Labour Party. She continued campaigning and, during the 1912 General Strike in Brisbane for the right to establish trade unions, Emma led a large contingent of women to Parliament House.

Emma died at Toowoomba on 22 January 1917. She was buried at Brisbane's Toowong Cemetery and was survived by one son.

Lady Mary Murray 1732-1765

Mary Dalton was the daughter of Richard Dalton of Banner Cross (Ecclesall), now part of Sheffield, and his wife Mary, née Bright. Her great grandfather was John Bright of Banner Cross, whose wife was Mary Youle of Chesterfield. After the deaths of her father, Alderman Richard Youle, and her brother Nicholas, she inherited that family's wealth. The couple lived in Chesterfield. They had five sons and four daughters. John died in 1734, aged 77 years. According to his will, John owned land in Walton, Hasland, Spittle (sic), Newbold and Matlock, and the house in Hollis Croft, where his son John lived, together with land in Yorkshire.

The only son to outlive John senior, was John junior, who married Barbara Jessop, daughter of Francis Jessop of

Broomhall, Sheffield. They had two daughters, Barbara, who died aged 24 years, after a brief marriage without children, and Mary, who married Richard Dalton. The couple had two children, Bright and Mary Dalton. Although John Bright senior made provision in his will for his daughters and grandchildren, his executor John junior, appears to have been negligent in paying some of the legacies, deferring payment during his lifetime with the promise of benefits after his death. However, when he died in April 1748, he left all his real and personal estate to his executor, Godfrey Heathcote, in trust for his grandson, Bright Dalton, whose parents had died. In the event of his decease before the age of 20 years, everything was to go to his sister Mary. Sadly, Bright died in August 1748 aged just 14, so everything passed to Mary. In 1750, an action was brought against the estate for the payment in full of the legacies left by John senior to his daughters and grandchildren. The case evidently dragged on, as probate was not granted until 1752. Godfrey Heathcote kept a book of accounts relating to the estate between 1748 and 1754, when presumably the estate was settled. Mentioned in the accounts were 'a payment to Miss Dalton a Portugal Piece value £3 12s 0d, in lieu of one, which the Testator formerly made a present of, for working him a waistcoat, but took back into his own money, when the Rebells were in Derbyshire [the 1745 Rebellion]' and £2 2s 0d for her pocket expenses on her going to a boarding school in York. Mary Dalton, aged just 22 years, was now a very wealthy young lady and held considerable property. The frontage of the land she owned on Holywell Street, today stretches from the University of Derby to Holywell House, together with the land behind reaching, almost to what is now Infirmary Road.

Lady Mary's property on Holywell Street, part of which has been renamed Sheffield Road. John Bright's house was the two storey-building in the centre.

When she married Lord John Murray in 1758, the *Derby Mercury* described her 'as a most agreeable lady with a fortune of £50,000' (over £5 million today), and according to the *Scots Magazine*, she was 'said to be an heiress of £2,000 p.a.' (£200,000 today). Mary was 26 and Lord John was 41. He was the son of the first Duke of Atholl by his second marriage. Two of his half-brothers, William and George, were leaders in the Jacobite Army in 1745. However, Lord John was a Member of Parliament, representing Perthshire between 1734 and 1761, as a supporter of the Whig party. He had a distinguished military career, serving as Colonel of the 42nd Highlanders (the Black Watch) for over 40 years, being promoted to General in 1770.

Lord and Lady Murray spent most of their time at Banner Cross Hall and London. A presence, however, was maintained in Chesterfield. John Bright's house would have been inadequate for the couple and their retinue, and a new house was probably started soon after their marriage. It would most likely have been completed by the time Lord John attended Chesterfield races in 1763, when it was possibly the scene of a grand social occasion. Most people would regard the house as a somewhat non-descript building adjacent to the former hospital, unaware that this is actually the rear of the building. It was built this way round in order to take advantage of the spectacular views over the valley of the Rother.

Holywell House

Sadly, Lady Mary died in London in 1765, and her body was brought back to Sheffield, where she was buried in the central aisle of Sheffield Parish Church (now the Cathedral), alongside her mother. The couple had a daughter, Mary. By her will, Lady Mary devised her freehold estates in Derbyshire and Yorkshire, but not the silver that had come to her from her mother, to the use of Lord John Murray for his life in trust for their daughter and her heirs. Although, in 1770, Lord John had executed deeds, in which he disclaimed all right to the property and goods of his lady, in 1778, he wished to consolidate the estate at Banner Cross, by purchasing land intermixed with that of the Banner Cross estate. To finance this, he was anxious to sell such detached parts of the estate that, it was thought, advisable to be sold. This included property in Chesterfield. In 1781, the new house, 'with a Coache-house, Stables and pleasant Gardens, situate in Chesterfield, late in the possession of Lord John Murray' was offered to let. It changed hands shortly afterwards.

Mary married William Foxlowe of Staveley, who adopted the name Murray, and Banner Cross Hall was rebuilt. It is now the head office of Henry Boot Ltd.

There is no way of knowing how much time Lady Murray spent in Chesterfield during her lifetime, but, without her, the striking building, now known as Holywell House, would not have been built.

Catherine Parry 1925-2009

Catherine Parry was the daughter of John Henry Parry and his wife Mabel. Her father died when she was just 13-years-old.

Catherine was brought up on the Boythorpe estate, and most likely went to William Rhodes infant and junior schools. She was still at school when war broke out. Like other local children, she would have spent many happy hours in Queen's Park. As well as the play equipment, there were glorious floral displays.

The first glasshouses were erected behind the pavilion in the Park in 1897, and the park keeper was authorised to purchase 2,000 plant pots for plant propagation for the displays in the Park and elsewhere. There were additional greenhouses at Tapton House, after the estate was given to the town by Charles Markham. The greenhouses were not open to the public but, in 1930, a conservatory was purchased for Queen's Park, where the displays could be inspected.

Some idea of the scale of operations comes from the report of the Parks Superintendent, Mr McIntosh, in April 1932:

'Approximately 25,000 summer flowering plants were propagated in Queen's Park for the embellishment of the flower beds and borders in various parks and open spaces ... The border of dahlias in the Queen's Park provided a most attractive feature. A display of flowering and foliage plants was maintained in the Conservatory at the Queen's Park throughout the year ... 300 trees and shrubs were planted out'.

In 1945, Catherine was awarded a 1st class teacher's preliminary certificate in school and cottage gardening by the Royal Horticultural Society. She joined the Parks Department of Chesterfield Borough Council in the 1950s.

Eventually, the glasshouses at Queen's Park were removed, and the work concentrated at Tapton. A popular feature in 1942, was the carpet bedding design for the 'Holidays at Home' planting scheme on the slope opposite the conservatory.

For many years, the bedding scheme there was prepared and designed by Catherine. The plants for the design came from the Tapton nursery, where cuttings were taken every year. Depending upon the design, between 4,000 and 8,000 plants would be used, and the whole scheme took about six months to prepare and plant out.

Catherine worked for the council for 31 years. When she retired, she received a meritorious certificate from the council. She may not have had the adventures that some of the other women in this collection had, but she was definitely a woman in a man's world.

Baroness Richardson of Calow 1938-

Kathleen Margaret Fountain was born in February 1938, the daughter of Francis and Margaret Fountain of Calow. She attended Calow Primary School (which at that time was opposite the church) and then St Helena School (formerly the Girls' High School). She left school with A-levels in English, History and Scripture to undergo a teacher-training course at Stockwell College, run by the British and Foreign School Society, in Bromley, Kent, where she gained her Teacher's Certificate.

The family worshipped at the Congregational Chapel in Calow (now the United Reformed Church), and Kathleen went three times on a Sunday. Having finished her teacher training, she became a teacher of Religious Education at Hollingwood Senior School near Chesterfield, from 1958-61. The local nonconformist church where she now lived, was a Methodist church, and she joined in the activities there, and became a local preacher and youth worker in 1959. After this, she trained as a deaconess at the Wesley Deaconess Institute at Ilkley, Yorkshire. In 1961, she was sent to work in Rochdale where she met the man who would become her husband. Since, at that time, the Wesley Deaconess Order did not allow married women, she had to resign and return to teaching. In 1964, she married Ian Richardson at Brimington Methodist Church; they had three daughters. When the Methodist Church decided to allow women to become ministers, Kathleen studied theology at Wesley House, Cambridge. In 1980, she was ordained and became the Revd Richardson ministering in the Denby Dale and Clayton West Circuit. In 1987 she became Chairman of the West Yorkshire District of the Methodist Church – the first woman to become the chair of a district. Later, in 1992, Kathleen became the first female to become the President of the Methodist

Conference, and during that year she preached at the United Reformed Churches at Chesterfield and Calow.

She became involved in the ecumenical movement, which seeks to develop closer relationships between the different church traditions. Firstly, she served as the Moderator of the Free Church Federal Council from 1995-9, as well as president of Churches Together in England. Later, she became Moderator of the Churches Commission on Inter-Faith Relationships.

In 1996, she received an OBE for her services to the ecumenical movement. She also received three honorary degrees: a Doctor of Divinity (Birmingham 1999); a Doctor of Laws (Liverpool 1997); and a Doctor of Letters (Bradford 1994). Kathleen was pleased to receive this public recognition of the work she had done from organisations outside the church.

In 1998, Kathleen was created a life peer, Baroness Richardson of Calow, sitting as an Independent Crossbench peer, until her retirement in 2018. She tended to speak on health and social care, immigration, education and moral/religious issues. She supported the case for assisted dying and same-sex marriages. Kathleen served on two Select Committees – one on the use of animals in scientific procedures; the other on religious offences, which considered the abolition of the blasphemy laws.

Based in London, she became a supernumerary minister in the London District of the Methodist Church, and is now based in the Enfield Circuit.

Kathleen lived in Calow until she was 18, but continued to

visit whilst her sister lived in Chesterfield. At the time, there were many miners in the village mostly employed at Arkwright and Markham collieries, although her father was an engineer at Staveley Coal & Iron Co. Most of the women were housewives. A popular meeting place was the Miner's Welfare, where Kathleen played snooker and tennis.

In 2010, Kathleen returned to Calow with Ruth Mcdonald, who was presenting a series *Lords A Visiting* to be broadcast on Radio 4 the following year. It featured members of the House of Lords visiting the titular land of their peerages. Whilst there, she visited the United Reformed Church, where she met old friends. Whilst at the replacement Calow School, she answered questions from the pupils' school council about her work in the House of Lords; she played bowls with over 65s at the local leisure centre behind Eastwood Park, and undertook knotting with the local scout troop (she had been a guide). Many men were unemployed, but a great number of women worked at the hospital.

When she was 80, Kathleen returned once more to meet up with four of the girls who started school with her.

Hannah Roberts 1798-1867

Hannah was the daughter of Henry Bradley and his wife Rebecca. Her uncle was Job Bradley, Post Master, printer, bookseller, and Mayor of Chesterfield in 1791. When he died, the business was taken over by his brother Henry and, after his death, by Henry's wife Rebecca, until her death in 1815, when Hannah took over at the age of 17. Having run the business for eight years, Hannah married John Roberts, Lieutenant of the Royal Navy, in 1823. Consequently he became the town's Post Master and took over the business.

John Roberts is given the credit for establishing the *Chesterfield Gazette*, which became the *Derbyshire Courier*. However, Hannah's obituary in the *Derbyshire Courier* on 30 November 1867, said that:

'As a corrector of the press she was almost unrivalled. Her quickness of observation and accuracy of detail enabled her often to contribute to the columns of this journal graphic sketches of passing events, and rapid expressions of public opinion'.

Although Hannah did the work, John got the credit.

Henry and Job Bradley had a sister, Isabella. She was the wife of John Bower, Mayor of Chesterfield, and agent for the French prisoners of war in the town. Hannah would have most likely visited their home at Spital Lodge as a child, and would have known General d'Henin, one of the prisoners who lived there whilst on parole. The *Derbyshire Courier* of 27 December 1845 contained an anonymous article about the French prisoners of war, which surely must have been written by Hannah. It is this article that gives us much of the information about the French prisoners of war in Chesterfield.

John and Hannah moved to Spital Lodge shortly before John's death in 1856. Hannah then ran the business, together with her son John, until 1867, when he was declared bankrupt. However, the bankruptcy was discharged when the company was sold. Shortly afterwards, Hannah died. Her daughter Isabella had been living with her and had, at some time, been the editor of the *Derbyshire Courier*. Once the contents of Spital Lodge had been sold, including five volumes of Chambers Dictionary, Isabella left Chesterfield to spend many years travelling in Europe, before returning to live in Chelsea, not far from her brother Henry, who had had a distinguished army career.

Florence 1888-1976, Cecile Bradbury 1893-1965 and Dorothy Robinson 1895-1985

Florence and her two younger sisters, Cecile and Dorothy, known to the family as Dolly, were the daughters of William Bradbury Robinson and his second wife Jane Davenport. They were also the granddaughters of John Robinson, who founded the company which became Robinson & Sons. When Florence was born, the family lived at Field House in Brampton. She was educated at Chesterfield Girls' High School, finishing her schooling at Clapham High School in London.

At the time of the 1911 census, Florence was staying in Violet Markham's house in Gower Street, London, together with Jessie Smith, the honorary secretary of the Chesterfield Society for Women's Suffrage, and Jessie's sister. Living a few doors away was Dame Millicent Garrett Fawcett, leader of the National Union of Women's Suffrage Societies.

When war broke out, two women doctors, Louisa Garrett Anderson and Flora Murray, who were prominent suffragettes, founded the Women's Hospital Corps, to care for wounded soldiers. The first hospital was originally in Paris but, after a change of policy, British casualties were evacuated to England rather than being treated in France. They were asked to run a large military hospital in London, and the hospitals in France were closed. The London hospital was opened in May 1915 in the old St Giles Union workhouse in Endell Street. It was near main line railway stations, which meant that it received a high proportion of severely injured soldiers. When convoys of casualties arrived at the hospital, sometimes bringing up to 80 men at a time, there could be as many as 30 needing immediate surgery. Although officially a military hospital, funded by the Army, the Hospital was largely ignored by the Royal Army Medical Corps. The Women's Hospital Corps was left to run it as they wished. It was staffed almost completely by women. The nursing staff initially comprised a matron, an assistant matron, 28 sisters and 60 nursing orderlies, who wore white overalls. It is probably about this time that Florence joined the hospital as, although press reports refer to her being a nursing orderly at Endell Street, there was no mention of her being in France. Her younger sister Dorothy was an orderly in the X-ray department. In 1918, the Representation of the People Act gave the vote to women aged over 30 who met minimum property qualifications. The hospital staff celebrated this event by hoisting the flag of the Women's Social and Political Union in the hospital's courtyard. Also, in 1918, the engagement of Dorothy to Captain Alexander Joseph Bell of the King's Royal Rifle Corps was announced. He was a prisoner of war for two years.

The hospital closed at the end of 1919, but Florence had returned to Chesterfield by then to join Robinson & Sons. A health department had been established there in 1918, and Florence was appointed Head of the Department in 1920. She was a pioneer and leading figure nationally in industrial welfare and personnel work, establishing a training school for new employees, instituting a holiday camp at Abergele, initially for girls but later for boys as well – and encouraging sports teams at the Walton Dam sports ground. She founded the firm's Operatic Society in 1922, directing performances until the outbreak of the Second World War. Standing as a Liberal, Florence was elected to the Borough Council in 1931 for Holmebrook Ward, which she represented for 24 years.

She was appointed Mayor in 1946 and Alderman in 1949. She also served as a Borough Magistrate and chairman of the Juvenile Court Panel. Sadly, she had to retire from the council and other duties in 1955 as a result of ill health.

Florence had been closely associated with the Settlement almost from her schooldays, and when it was reorganised in 1942, she became the Chairman of the Executive Committee.

In 1911, Cecile and Dorothy were at Cheltenham Ladies' College, finishing their education.

Cecile became a VAD during WWI, working initially at Ashgate Hospital, where her mother Jane, at that time, was working as a cook. The First Aid Nursing Yeomanry (FANY) was founded in 1909. Unlike nursing organisations, the FANY saw themselves rescuing the wounded and giving first aid on the way to the field hospitals. The British Army wanted nothing to do with them, as it was thought that the Front was no place for women. As a result, they drove ambulances and ran hospitals and casualty clearing stations for the Belgian and French Armies. As soon as she was 23, Cecile applied to join the

FANY as a VAD. At the end of 1916, the French Société de Secours aux Blessés Militaire (SSBM) asked the FANY to establish a hospital at Port à Binson, on the Marne just to the west of Verdun and close to the French border. This turned out to be in an old priory, which was very dirty and neglected, and the advance party spent a month cleaning it. In February 1917, Cecile was one of the nurses posted to the hospital. With its site on a hillside and a view over the valley, Cecile would have found it a pleasant place to be if it were not for the constant roar of the big guns just a short distance away.[7] The first wounded from around Verdun arrived on 19 March; eventually there were 200 French patients.

There were about 360 members of FANY. They received many decorations for bravery, including 17 Military Medals, 1 Legion d'Honneur, and 27 Croix de Guerre. Cecile received the Medaille de Société aux Blessés Militaire (which eventually became the French Red Cross), as did some of the nurses who had travelled out from England at the same time.

After the war ended, Cecile underwent nurse's training at St Thomas' Hospital in London, where she spent seven years before joining the Overseas Dominions Nursing Service, spending three years at a hospital in Tanganyika (now Tanzania). She returned to Chesterfield at the end of 1928, before going to Hong Kong. She was at home in Chesterfield for Christmas 1938 for the first time in ten years before returning to Hong Kong the following August, where in 1940 she was matron of the cholera hospital.

The British colony of Hong Kong surrendered to Japanese forces on Christmas Day 1941. In anticipation of trouble, women and children had been ordered to leave Hong Kong on ships provided, but career and auxiliary nurses were excluded from the order. After an appalling interlude spent in former brothels

7. https://www.fany.org.uk/history/wwi/overview

and squalid tenements along the waterfront, approximately 2800 men, women and children were transported on 20-21 January to the relatively isolated Stanley peninsula on the south east coast of Hong Kong Island. Except for the removal of unburied corpses, the internees found that very little had been done to prepare the camp for their arrival. 'There were no cooking facilities, no furniture, little crockery or cutlery; toilet facilities were filthy, shamefully inadequate, and without water. Living space was cramped and grossly inadequate'. Medical facilities were almost non-existent. It was tragic for nurses like Cecile, but fortunately the presence of some forty doctors and 100 trained nurses in the hospital and clinics, which were established, prevented any major epidemics ocuring. Malaria, malnutrition and its associated diseases, beriberi and pellagra, were the most common ailments, but not cholera.[8]

It was not until late September 1942 that her mother received a message that she was safe, although interned. Eventually, in January 1944, her mother received a couple of postcards and a letter from Cecile, in which she said she was well and allowed to bathe in the sea. On 16 August 1945, the Japanese surrendered. Cecile finally returned home in November 1945, although the arrival was delayed by storms. Florence met her. However, when she reached home, she retired to bed with bronchitis.

It was hardly surprising that she retired from nursing and, a year later, Florence asked her to be her Mayoress.

Dorothy and Alex were married in 1920. He became the manager of Robinson & Sons London Office in Old Street, and the couple lived in Baron's Court. On 11 Sep 1940, a bomb fell in the street near their home. Fortunately, Dorothy and Alex were at the rear of the house and were unharmed, but the house was badly damaged. When Alex phoned the office to ask them to send a van to collect their important belongings, he learned that

8. Bernice Archer & Fedorowich Kent (1996). The women of Stanley: internment in Hong Kong 1942–45, Women's History Review, 5:3, 373-399

a huge bomb had fallen through the basement lights of the warehouse, but fortunately it didn't explode. The top two floors of the office block, not used by Robinson & Sons, were destroyed and the Robinson's offices below were rendered useless by water. The typewriters were rescued and taken to a shop to be repaired but, before they could be collected, it too was destroyed by a bomb. Another office was found in High Holborn. Alex remained in London whilst Dorothy returned to Chesterfield, where she was active with the Women's Voluntary Service (WVS), an organiser of the Chesterfield Services canteen unit, as well as being secretary and later manager of the Kit Bag Club.

A monument in Old Brampton churchyard marks the burial place of their father, William Bradbury Robinson, in 1911, his second wife Jane in 1950, Florence in 1976, and their younger brother Victor Owen and his wife. Cecile was cremated. Dorothy died in Oxfordshire. Their elder brother was Sir Robert Robinson, a Nobel Prize winner for Chemistry.

Susan Shentall 1934-1996

Susan Shentall was born on 21 May 1934, the daughter of John Shentall, owner of a chain of grocers and provision merchants, and his wife Gwendoline. In 1939, the family was living at Old Brampton.

In 1940, she was attending St Joseph's High School, where she passed a London Guildhall Drama and Art Examination in elementary elocution, something which later would be of great benefit to her. She enjoyed watching sport, studying paintings, and reading poetry.

After leaving school, she took a domestic science course followed by a sixth month stay in Paris with a French family, before embarking on a shorthand typing course in London, with the idea that she might become a journalist. Her family visited her in London in March 1953. They were dining in a restaurant, when the owner asked the young lady, with honey-blonde hair and blue eyes, if he could let the producer of the film *Romeo and Juliet* know she was there, as they were looking for someone to take the part of Juliet. The film was to be directed by Renato Castellani. It was to be shot in Technicolor in Verona. To see if she was suitable, Susan was given a film test at Pinewood Studios.

The following Monday, she went to the Rank Headquarters, where it was confirmed that she had got the part. A hectic week ensued, starting with a meeting with the dressmaker, followed by a two-hour press conference, after which she was featured in many papers. The next day was spent in conference with the producer and film executives. Fortunately, her father was an experienced businessman when it came to negotiating contracts, as Susan would have no experience of such things. In the evening there was a family party to celebrate. On Wednesday, her first visit to the studio was followed by six hours with the hair dresser. Then came a reception with the overseas executives, as the film was a joint venture between Rank and Universalcine. On Thursday, there were tests with different make-ups, followed by an attendance at a film premier, and then a party at the restaurant where she had been discovered. Friday saw more make-up tests with Laurence Harvey, who was to play Romeo. Then it was back to Chesterfield, where she packed for her first trip to Italy. She stayed near Lake Garda. Filming took place in five centres including Verona, Venice and Rome.

In May 1954, she was back at Old Brampton, where she married Philip Worthington, son of the owner of a grocery chain in Leicester. The film was released in September 1954. Susan was regarded as a great success. She received many offers, including the chance to replace Grace Kelly who was marrying Prince Rainier, but she regarded the filming of *Romeo and Juliet* as a bit of fun and had no wish to continue in films, being quite happy to become a housewife. She had three children and died at Market Harborough, in 1996, after a long illness.

Elizabeth Simon 1933-2013

Joyce Elizabeth, usually known as Elizabeth, was the daughter of John Chester Simon and his second wife Mabel, née Austin, who was 19 years younger than her husband. They lived on Gladstone Road. Both Elizabeth's parents were Licentiates of the Royal Academy of Music, examinations which could be taken externally at that time. The couple performed regularly, and her father was organist at St Thomas' Brampton for 27 years. Elizabeth could play the piano at the age of three, the violin at five and the viola at eight. She was a contemporary of Susan Shentall at St Joseph's High School, where she passed a London Guildhall Drama and Art Examination in elocution, and the preliminary grade for the Associated Board of the Royal Academy and the Royal College of Music. She continued her education at Harrogate College.

Elizabeth entered the Royal Academy of Music in 1951 as a singer. During her time there she won several awards and prizes, also reaching diploma standard in the playing of the piano, violin and viola. She was chosen to represent the

Academy at a concert in Antwerp in 1956. The same year, she was one of two winners of the first competition for the prestigious Royal Philharmonic Society's Katherine Ferrier Award worth £300. The award was sufficient to cover the cost of a year's study and general support. She continued with her training in London, Paris and Munich. She could perform songs in German, French and Italian.

In November 1953, Elizabeth Simon (soprano) joined the Canterbury Choral Society in a performance of *Tom Jones*, by Edward German, in the Chapter House at Canterbury Cathedral. Sadly, her father died in 1954, just as her career was beginning. In June 1955, she took part in a performance of Mendelsohn's *A Midsummer Night's Dream* at the Dome, Brighton, along with the London Philharmonic and members of the Royal Academy of Dramatic Art.

In 1958, she entered the International Vocalists Contest in Holland, where she won a first prize and a prize for the best vocalist in the competition. She was competing with 98 singers from 18 countries.

Throughout her career, as well as performing on radio and television, she appeared in cathedrals and chapels, piers and pavilions, as well as appearing at festivals and the Eisteddfod. In 1963, she performed at the Promenade Concerts at the Albert Hall. She took part in broadcast recitals and *Friday Night is Music Night*. She also added Welsh to her repertoire.

Locally, she performed at

Alfreton (1965), Sheffield City Hall (1966) and, on 29 July 1967, she performed at the Parish Church, in a recital with Katie Bacon.

Eventually, Elizabeth returned to live at the family home on Gladstone Road. She married late in life. Joyce Elizabeth Gillard died in 2013. Like her parents, she was buried in Brimington Cemetery.

Hannah Smith 1856-1966

Hannah Smith was born in Broughton, Manchester in 1856, the daughter of a warehouseman. Her mother died when Hannah was young, so her grandmother came to live with the family until her father married again, and another sister, Catherine Mary, was born. Hannah went to the Manchester Municipal Technical College, where she gained a Diploma and a City and Guilds certificate in dressmaking.

By 1901, she had moved to Clay Cross with her sister Catherine, who was a teacher at Clay Cross Girls' School, originally as a mistress in the junior girls' school and later in the senior girls' school. In January the same year, Hannah was teaching an evening class in dressmaking at Clowne Girls' School. She was employed by the Derbyshire County Council Technical Education Committee. The course was to last for 12 weeks. Hannah was described as having excellent qualifications, as well as being capable and resourceful. When she taught a course at Osmaston by Ashbourne, the course was so popular that she was asked to return a couple of years later. At the time of the 1911 census, the sisters were still living in Clay Cross, and she was described as a teacher of scientific dressmaking. She was said to have travelled everywhere by pony and trap or train.

In 1939, both sisters had retired and they were living on Ashgate Road, where Hannah spent many happy hours in her garden. She remained on Ashgate Road until a few years before her death, when she moved to a home in Sheffield, after a spell in Scarsdale Hospital. When she celebrated her 100th birthday, she was visited by the Lord Mayor and Lady Mayoress of Sheffield and the Mayor and Mayoress of Chesterfield, and enjoyed a cake made for her by a neighbour on Ashgate Road. Unfortunately the party for her 110th birthday had to be cancelled, but she managed a sip of champagne. At the time of her death shortly afterwards in January 1966, Hannah Smith was the oldest living person in the country.

Jessie Smith 1886- ?

Jessie was the eldest daughter of Frederick Smith and his wife Jennie. Frederick was a dental surgeon on Burlington Street. His two sons, Harold and Frederick, were also dental surgeons. In 1911, they were living at Grove Hill, Newbold. Jessie, however, was staying with her sister and Florence Robinson in Violet Markham's house in Gower Street, London. In 1913, she was living with her brother Harold on Walton Road.

Jessie was a member of the Chesterfield Students' Association and attended the University Extension Lectures. She was awarded a scholarship to the value of £7 to attend the summer school at Oxford in 1903. She was a supporter of the Newbold Continuation School and the Whittington Women's Adult School.

On 18 November 1910, there were violent scenes outside the Houses of Parliament, when Prime Minister Asquith refused to allow time to consider the Parliamentary Franchise (Women's)

Bill. Along with Winifred Jones, Jessie Smith was among the 117 people arrested, but she was released without charge.

A Chesterfield branch of the National Union Women's Suffrage Societies was formed by 1912. In July the following year, the Pilgrims associated with the NUWSS visited Chesterfield on their way from Newcastle to London. Two drays were placed in the Market Place to serve as platforms, the principal one being occupied by Councillor Harry Cropper and Mrs (later Dame) Millicent Fawcett. There was also a meeting in the Market Hall. It was proclaimed that the Pilgrims were opposed to violence and, although the square was packed, the crowd was good natured, listening to the speakers attentively. The committee of the Chesterfield branch of the NUWSS at the time included Jessie Smith and Alice Stevens. (See Marie Louise Wilkes and Alice Stevens)

In November 1913, a students' association was formed in connection with the Chesterfield branch of the NUWSS. The first speaker was Jessie, who spoke about the economic position of women in the home.

In December 1913, Mrs Snowden, a member of the executive of the NUWSS, visited Chesterfield. Her speech at the Market Hall was well received. The following March, it was the turn of Miss Maude Royden, another member of the executive. Eight dozen copies of *Common Cause* (the NUWSS magazine) were sold at the meeting and a further dozen in the street outside.

For the Chesterfield Shopping Week in April 1914, Jessie proposed to mount an exhibition on sweated labour, showing the conditions under which women worked, hidden in the slums. In May, she spoke to the Congregational and Social Union on the *Emancipation of Women*. She spoke at an open meeting in Staveley in August. At the AGM in June, Jessie was able to report that the Chesterfield Branch had 100 members and

200 'Friends'. As well as the major meetings, there were 'cottage meetings' held at her home, Walton Rise, and Red House Brampton.

In February 1917, the Royal Sanitary Institute held a conference on Infant Welfare Work in Chesterfield. Jessie gave a resume of the work done in West Ward and arranged an exhibition relating to the clinic held there. She also asked for an enforcement of the by-laws regarding smoke nuisance, which was particularly bad in that area. She said that enforcement would save women a lot of time spent in clearing away dirt and unnecessary washing.

Having got that out of the way, she was a member of the Infant Welfare and Public Health sub-committee, arranging the Civic and Industrial Exhibition held in April, as part of the traders' effort to raise funds for the hospital, the success of which enabled the hospital to add 'Royal' to its name.

In July 1918, Jessie married Charles Henry Davies at the Registry Office. Sadly, that is the last we hear of her. Her husband was not a local man.

Rose Smith 1891-1985

Rosina Ellis was born in Putney on 10 May 1891, the daughter of Samuel Ellis and his wife Sarah Ann. Like his father, Samuel was a thrower in the pottery industry. He grew up in Lambeth, where their first son Percy was born.

After the birth of Rosina, the family moved to Glamorgan, where Thomas was born, and then to Clifton, Gloucestershire, where Sarah Ann had been born and where Rosina's brother Joseph was born. They finally arrived in Chesterfield about 1899.

The family lived on Sanforth Street, Whittington. Samuel was likely to have been employed at Pearson's pottery on Whittington Moor.

The children began their education at the Whittington Moor Endowed School. In 1901, Percy won a scholarship to continue his education at Clay Cross Science School, as did Rosina in 1903, and Thomas in 1905. (At that time Whittington was not part of Chesterfield.) At Chesterfield Teachers' Centre, she obtained a preliminary certificate, which enabled her to gain employment as an elementary school teacher at Newbold St John's Church of England Infant School.

Early 20th Century housing in Chesterfield. Sanforth Street would have originally looked like this.

About 1910, Rosina joined the Social Democratic Federation, which had been active in Chesterfield since 1905. The Federation condemned the Labour candidates at the General Election of 1910, who had previously been Liberals, saying that they were not truly committed to Labour's cause. In Chesterfield, the Federation called upon the miners to vote against Haslam, but he was returned to Parliament.

Rosina continued her education with the Workers' Education Association, which was based at the Toynbee Room within the Settlement building. Her lecturers were part of the Oxford University Extension Scheme. In 1913 and 1914, she attended a summer school at Balliol College, Oxford. Although she was offered a place at Lady Margaret College to train as a WEA lecturer, she did not take it, as she felt that being a WEA lecturer and her Marxist views were incompatible.

In 1916, Rosina married Alfred H. Smith. He was two years older than Rosina and had been a lodger in nearby Wharf Lane.

He was a sign writer before war broke out. As the wedding was at Windsor, where there was an army barracks, he may have been in the army. As Rosina was now married, she had to leave her teaching job, something she resented. She found a job doing war work at Robinson & Sons, where she became a voluntary trade union leader.

After the war, the couple lived in Chesterfield, where, in 1920, their twin sons were born, but shortly afterwards they moved to Mansfield, where Rosina joined the Socialist Labour Party, a far-left splinter group from the Socialist Democratic Federation. In 1922, the whole group joined the Communist Party of Great Britain (CPGB), which had been established in 1920. Now Rosina was usually referred to as 'Rose' in the press. She became closely involved with the CPGB, becoming the National Women's Organiser.[9] She also became prominent during the unrest surrounding the 1926 general strike, when she opened her home to miners' activists as a distribution and agitation centre. In June, she was fined 4gns 'for making a speech likely to cause disaffection among the civilian population'. She also campaigned for additional relief for the families of the strikers. In 1929, she was selected to stand for the communists in the general election, receiving just 533 votes.

By 1930, the marriage between Rose and Alfred had broken down. Alfred moved to Worksop, where he was in business as a sign writer and painter. The boys went with Rose, but, in 1939, both boys were employed as house painters like their father.

Rose turned her attention to Burnley, where there was considerable disruption amongst the cotton weavers. In 1930, she organised the women's contingent, which travelled separately, but formed part of the march associated with the national hunger strike. A group from Burnley travelled to Bradford, where they met a contingent from Yorkshire and

9. For full details of Rose's activities see Gisela Chan Man Fong PhD: The life and times of Rose Smith in Britain and China 1891-1985. https://spectrum. library.concordia.ca/469/1/NQ44808.pdf

marched, via Leeds and Wakefield, to Sheffield, where they caught a train to Luton before marching to join a rally in Hyde Park on May Day. They carried a large red banner bearing the slogan 'To the textile workers of Yorkshire from the textile workers of Moscow'.

In 1931, Rose was selected to stand in the General Election in Burnley. A few days before the election, she was involved in scenes of disorder. At the ensuing trial she said:

"I came to Burnley at the invitation of the local group of the Communist Party to run as their candidate in the forthcoming election. I submit that from first coming to Burnley I have been under police surveillance."

She had taken lodgings in Burnley, but gave her permanent address as London. She was sentenced to three months' hard labour, which she served at Strangeways, 'in respect of inciting people to interfere with the police'. She was replaced as candidate at Burnley, but stood at Mansfield where, once more, she received 533 votes.

After standing unsuccessfully in a by-election for a place on Burnley council, when she gave her occupation as teacher, Rose moved to London, where she became a journalist for the *Daily Worker*. One of her assignments was to report on the Spanish Civil War.

Rose retired from the *Daily Worker* in 1955, returning to Chesterfield where members of her family were still living. She helped organise the local branch of the Campaign for Nuclear Disarmament. In 1960, she went to Australia to live with her son Percy and his family, but she couldn't settle there. In 1961, she went to China, where the Chinese wanted to recruit an experienced journalist in Beijing. She worked for the Foreign

Languages Press and later for the Xinhua News Agency. This was at the time of the Sino-Soviet split over ideology, and her adoption of Maoism lost her friends in the CPGB, who were following the Soviet ideology. The Cultural Revolution began in 1966, and two years later, she returned to Chesterfield, as some of her friends and colleagues were being imprisoned. At the request of Zhou Enlai, premier of the People's Republic of China, she returned to China in 1971. A birthday party was held for her 90th birthday in Peking's (Beijing's) Great Hall of the People. She kept in touch with her family and, when she died in 1985, both her sons were with her. She was buried in the Revolutionary Martyrs' Cemetery in Beijing.

In an article in the *Peking Review* of 21 July 1967, Rose said that:

'The struggle among the masses had been my life blood' and 'Born of the British working class, reared among miners and textile workers, daily participating in the hardships and humiliations of their lives, it was there that I early learnt that the only way out for the working class is through proletarian revolution and the overthrow of capitalism.'

Margaret Stovin 1756-1846

Margaret Stovin was baptised at St George's Church, Doncaster on 3 January 1756, the daughter of James Stovin and his wife Margaret, née Whitaker. She was the fourth of five children. The first born, James, died young, a second James became the rector of Rossington, Yorkshire, although he spent much of his time in London; Mary married and went to live in London. The younger brother Richard joined the army and spent much of his time overseas. Their mother died in 1769 when Margaret was 12, but her father did not remain a widower for long as, in 1770, he married Theodosia Sparrow of Wincobank (Sheffield). A further six children were born including, John Sparrow, Lydia Theodosia, and Sarah Caroline who, in 1797, married Sir Sitwell Sitwell of Renishaw Hall, after Sitwell's first wife had died, leaving three children including a daughter Anne, who married Frederick, the youngest member of the Stovin family, who also joined the army.

After the death of her husband in 1789, Theodosia went to live in Birmingham, but in a codicil dated 1820 attached to her will of 1808, she left five guineas to the poor of Newbold, and she may have been living there with Lydia and Margaret at that time. The house had extensive grounds and is thought to have stood at the junction of Newbold Road and what is now Ulverstone Road. Theodosia died in 1834 at Newbold and was buried in the graveyard of St Lawrence Church, Barlow.

On several occasions, the sisters provided treats for the Newbold school children. In 1838, the children from the Newbold Sunday school were treated to an ample supply of buns, and each child was presented with a medal relating to Queen Victoria's coronation, largely at the expense of the Stovin family. Three years later, it was the turn of the day school, when the children (80 in number) assembled together at the request of Mrs M. Stovin[10] to commemorate the christening of the Princess Royal,

> 'after being very bountifully regaled with tea and excellent plum-cakes, the children went in procession with their banner and promenaded in that benevolent lady's grounds. After singing and giving three cheers for Queen Victoria, they thanked their kind benefactress, and returned to the school, and spent the evening in play and innocent diversions'.

10. Mrs is an honorary title – Margaret did not marry.

The sisters took part in Chesterfield's social activities. They attended a ball to raise funds for the Chesterfield Dispensary at the Angel Inn and they contributed funds towards the refurbishment of the organ at Chesterfield Parish Church. In 1841, Margaret was entertained at Sutton Hall by Robert Arkwright, along with others including the Duke of Rutland and the Marquis of Granby.

In 1836, the *Derby Mercury* reported the success of Margaret at an exhibition of the Chesterfield Floral and Horticultural Society, where there was

'a selection of very choice articles, particularly in the fruit department, in which the most successful competitor was Mrs M. Stovin; the uncommon fineness of her pears, plums, and apples surprised everyone, as well as the excellent vegetables, which were of decided merit'.

In 1829, the sisters donated some books to the library of the recently-formed Chesterfield Mechanics' Institute. As ladies attended the first meeting of the Institute the previous year, it seems likely that the sisters attended the meetings. One of the founder members of the Institute was Dr Jonathan Stokes. He was a highly-respected physician, botanist, and member of the Lunar Society, who had been living in Chesterfield since 1794, first on Lordsmill Street, and then in New Square, where he had a garden extending back to Saltergate. In his *Botanical Commentaries*, published in 1830, Dr Stokes made several references to a Newbold garden on gritstone, cultivated by Mrs M. Stovin 'an investigator and collector of plants'. Unfortunately, he died the following year, but he would have been able to encourage Margaret's interest in botany.

The Stovin family had connections with the Shore/

Nightingale family and, in 1833, Margaret presented Florence Nightingale with a herbarium (an album of pressed flowers and ferns), which the pair had collected, with most coming from Margaret's garden at Newbold, Lea Hurst, the home of the Nightingale family, the garden at Renishaw, and the garden at Rempstone Hall in Nottinghamshire. Sarah Caroline's husband, Sitwell, died in 1814. In 1820, the widowed Lady Sitwell married John Smith Wright Esq., of Nottingham, a widower with several children, but she still retained her former name and title of Lady Sitwell. A few years afterwards (about 1825), Mr Smith Wright and his family hired Rempstone Hall. Lady Sitwell continued to reside there until her death.

A page from the herbarium[11]

11. *An illustration from the Catalogue of the pressed flowers in the herbarium given to Florence Nightingale by Margaret Stovin in 1833. By Richard Mendelsohn MA MBA Bsc. Short Publishing Company Ltd. ISBN 978-1-899459-04-9*

Margaret built up a herbarium of her own of 1900 specimens. In July 1839, the house of Mrs Stovin, at Newbold, was broken into through the cellar window. Some silver items and several French gold coins were stolen. All the cabinet drawers were found rummaged, papers examined, and collection of autographs were thrown on the floor. Fortunately, the collection for her herbarium survived.

Margaret and Lydia remained at Newbold at least until the 1841 census. In 1843, the bank, Parker Shore and Company of Sheffield, went bankrupt. Lydia lost £1563 and her brother John Sparrow Stovin lost £396. This may be the reason for the sale of the property, which now belonged to John Sparrow The sisters moved to Ashgate, where sadly Margaret died of peritonitis in 1846. She left all her property to Lydia.

Lydia died on 14 May 1860, and Sarah Caroline died in November the same year, which is possibly why Margaret's herbarium passed to her niece Frances, daughter of her eldest brother James, who married James Worsley Pennyman. It was ultimately passed to Lt Colonel J. B. Pennyman of Ormesby Hall, Middlesbrough, who, in 1922, donated it to the Dorman Museum in Middlesbrough. The 1900 specimens are divided into two major sections – British wild species (20 volumes) and planted exotics (10 Volumes).

Mary Swanwick 1841-1917

Mary Swanwick was born at Old Whittington on 13 July 1841 the daughter of Frederick Swanwick and his wife Elizabeth née Drayton. She had a younger brother Russell, who left Whittington to become a farm manager at Cirencester.

The Swanwicks lived at Whittington House at Old Whittington (now demolished). Frederick was assistant to

George Stephenson. He regarded education as very important,
and was a great benefactor to the schools at Old Whittington,
New Whittington, and Whittington Moor. Mary continued the
work her father started, regularly visiting the schools as is
evidenced by entries in the school log books. She was one of the
managers of the Whittington Schools, which belonged to the
Webster Trustees, until the County Council took control. In 1930,
Eric Drayton Swanwick gave two fields adjacent to Old
Whittington School for the use as a recreation ground for the
children, in memory of his aunt. Shortly afterwards, the school
was renamed the Mary Swanwick Infant and Junior School.

Mary was a member of the Derbyshire County Council
Education Committee and the Chesterfield and District Higher
Education Committee. She was on the governing body of the
Chesterfield Girls' High School, where one of the houses was
named Swanwick in her memory, and a Mary Swanwick
Memorial Scholarship established.

Like her father, she was a supporter of the Oxford University
Extension Lectures on a wide range of subjects.

In 1894, she was persuaded to stand for election to the Board
of Guardians to represent Whittington Parish. In her election
address, she asked for votes as:

'duties of the Guardians include work which is pre-eminently
women's work. In carrying out arrangements for the right
bringing up of children, for the care of the sick, for dealing with
the aged and infirm, whether outside or inside the workhouse,
the responsible co-operation of women should be of real
service'.

She also suggested that the addition of women to the Boards
of Guardians elsewhere had improved their efficiency and the

economy of their administration, thereby reducing costs. As Whittington had been her place of birth and residence, the voters could be assured that she would have the interests of the parish at heart. She was a member for 20 years.

One of the people to benefit from her interest was Joseph Syddall, whom she sponsored to attend the Herkomer School of Art in Bushey, Hertfordshire. He became a well-known artist. Chesterfield Museum has a collection of his paintings.

In December 1900, Mary had a distressing experience when she visited London. On arriving at St Pancras, she took a cab to Portman Square to deliver a parcel. A man opened the cab door for her and, having rung the bell, she asked him to bring the parcel that she had left in the cab. He did so, but to her surprise, when she turned to tip him he was already walking away. She asked the cab driver to go after him but when she put her hand in her pocket, her purse had gone. A cry of 'Stop thief' by someone alerted a local policeman who gave chase and caught the man, with Mary's purse containing £1 16s in his hand. On being taken to court the following day, he was identified as someone who had been charged a short while ago with begging at cab doors and assaulting policemen. He was sentenced to two months' hard labour.

The Mary Swanwick memorial at Elder Yard Unitarian Chapel

Mary was also a member of Chesterfield Civic Guild. She died on 7 April 1917. Her obituary in the *Derbyshire Courier* of 17 April was headed 'A life of public service'. Like her father, she worshipped at Elder Yard Unitarian Chapel, as did her nephew Eric Drayton Swanwick. Mary was interred in Spital Cemetery

Rhoda Tattersall 1902-1993

Rhoda Tattersall was the daughter of Thomas and Sarah Hannah Tattersall. Thomas was a policeman, who later became a county court bailiff. Rhoda had a younger sister Elsie and, in 1925, the two sisters were running a confectioner's business on Wharf Lane. The following year, Rhoda began her nurse's training at the Royal Hospital, qualifying in 1929, and becoming a ward sister in 1935, as well as qualifying as a midwife. In January 1939, she left Chesterfield to take up a post at the Royal Hospital Baghdad, where she was employed by the Iraq government. She probably had doubts about the wisdom of the move, as, in April, King Ghazi of Iraq died following a car crash. There were rumours of a conspiracy. An angry crowd gathered outside the embassy at Mosul where the British Consul was brutally murdered.

In April 1941, there was a coup d'état, and Rashid Ali Al Gaylani seized power. He attempted to remove British influence from Iraq, seeking instead to negotiate settlements with the Axis powers. The small air bases at Basra and Habbaniyah were in danger. The resulting military action continued until the end of May. It must have been a worrying time for her family until they knew she was safe. A letter to her sister Elsie was published in the *Derbyshire Times* of 19 Sep 1941 telling of her experiences. When military action began on 29 April, all the women were told they would be transported to the Habbaniyah air base, so that they could be transported to Basra, and then on to India. The nurses at the hospital decided to remain behind, but, the following day, all British citizens were told to go to the Embassy for protection. They had to leave everything behind. Rhoda continued:

'The mob of people round the gate, shouting and bawling was not pleasant believe me. The Iraqis took our wireless transmitting set, so we could not send messages to Habbaniyah – also as many rifles as they could find. So we were left to sandbag ourselves in. ... There were 300 people in our place, so there was plenty to do. We started a surgery in case of accidents, a canteen had to be run, hygiene to attend to and a defence corps to be organised. Everywhere had to be sprayed twice a day to keep away the mosquitoes.'

Fortunately, the anticipated support from the Germans for the rebels did not come, but it was not until the end of May that an armistice was signed, and the prisoners finally released from the Embassy after four weeks.

Their houses had been ransacked. The microscope and all the results of the research work of her fiancé Dr Arnold Mills had been removed. Nothing more is known of her fiancé. Rhoda also said that she had just received a copy of the *Derbyshire Times* dated the previous November.

Rhoda remained at the hospital at least until 1943, but, according to the Nursing Register, she was working for the Anglo Iranian Oil Company in 1946. The same year, she decided to return permanently to England. She arrived at Liverpool on 26 May on board the *Orbita* of the Pacific Steam Navigation from Port Said. She made her way to Mansfield to stay with her sister Elsie. She no longer appears in the Nursing Register, so, presumably, she gave up nursing. Nothing more is known until she was living in Cheltenham in 1969, which is where her death was registered in 1993 at the age of 91. Possibly, her sister had gone to join Rhoda, as her death was also registered there in 1999, at the age of 93.

Greta Walker 1898-1973

Mary Greta Walker (usually known as Greta) was born on 25 May 1898, the only daughter of Frederick Arthur Walker and his wife Jemima Christian, née Warters. Frederick was a solicitor in the partnership Stanton and Walker. They lived at Woodside on Ashgate Road (now the Woodside public house). Greta attended Chesterfield Girls' High School, moving from the original building at East Bank to the new building on Sheffield Road.

From school, Greta went to Newnham College, Cambridge, where, in 1918, she obtained a Modern Languages Tripos. Perhaps, she had been encouraged to go there by Miss Stevens, (see Marie Louise Wilkes and Alice Stevens).

Greta returned to Chesterfield and, in 1920, she was one of the prize winners for the most original and attractive costume in a fancy dress competition at a reunion dance for past and present students in the upper classes of the Girls' High School.

She became treasurer of the Workers' Educational Association and took part in play readings at the Settlement.

Greta then set off on her travels. Following her visit to the Panama Canal, she gave a talk called *Off the Beaten Track* about the experience on the radio station 2LO. In August 1932, she was appointed secretary to the British Minister in Addis Ababa. An article in the *Birmingham Gazette,* dated 1 August 1935 described her shopping expedition to the market:

'the grocer is Greek, the pork butcher German, the dressmaker Italian, the (lady) coal merchant Armenian, the tailor Goanese, the nouveaute (novelty) dealer Russian and the carpenter Indian. French is the universal language but French as she is spoken by Slavs, Teutons or Semites is continents away from Anglo Saxon sixth-form French'. ... Arriving home 'there is a young Chinese waiting with kimonos and pyjamas and an old Ethiopian curio dealer delighting my small daughter with pictures showing in distressingly full detail that popular old Ethiopian legend, the love story of Solomon and the Queen of Sheba!'

This is the only mention of a child, although in the National Register of 1939, there is an unnamed juvenile living at Woodside. Greta would have had to leave Ethiopia in 1935 when Fascist Italian forces invaded the country.

She was back in Chesterfield by July 1936, when she gave a talk about her visit to Persia to the Chesterfield Ladies' Luncheon Club at the Picture House restaurant. She is also known to have visited the West Indies and Czechoslovakia – a well-travelled lady!

At the beginning of December 1939, a Soldiers' Reception Committee was established in Chesterfield with the intention of establishing canteens and social centres, arranging indoor and outdoor sports and organising concerts, dances, and entertainments for soldiers stationed in the town. The aim was to effect an introduction between the soldiers and local families. The secretaries were Greta and Mary Woodhead. They ran the Kit Bag Club, which was established at 55 Low Pavement (behind where Greggs now stands). It was officially opened at the end of the month.

The club supplied books (especially thrillers) and magazines.

There were refreshments, a wireless, a gramophone, and a games room with table tennis, darts and a bagatelle board, and a room with note paper so that the men were able to write home.

As well as running the club, there were events to be organised to raise funds, including boxing matches, dances, and whist drives. The club was so successful that, in 1944, it was said to have been extended four times.

If organising the Kit Bag Club wasn't enough Greta was a full-time ARP warden, in charge of salvage collection for the WVS, and, in 1940, she was appointed a magistrate.

Her time in Chesterfield came to an end in 1943. Captain Alexander Thomson was stationed in Chesterfield for three months in 1941, and it was presumably then that he met Greta at the Kit Bag Club. Also, in 1941, his first wife died aged 48; at the time he was said to be abroad. His eldest son Alexander died suddenly aged 19, on 13 April 1943. Two weeks later, on 30

April, Alexander and Greta were married by special licence in Edinburgh. It must have been a difficult time for Greta, as her parents sold Woodside in May, and she had to say goodbye to all her friends, colleagues as well as her very busy life in Chesterfield. After that, she left for Forres on the coast 25 miles north east of Inverness in June 1943.

Alexander died on 5 January 1973 and Greta a month later on 11 February. The couple were buried in Cluny Hill Cemetery, Forres.

Dorothy Webster 1906-1997

Dorothy Webster was the daughter of Mr A. E. Webster, who was born in Bradford. He came to Chesterfield in 1916 to become the manager of the lithographic printing department at Robinson & Sons, Portland Works. In 1918, he became the editor and manager of the *Link* (Robinson & Sons house magazine).

Dorothy became a student at Chesterfield School of Art. At the Arts and Crafts exhibition held by the school in September 1928, she won the first prize for Industrial Design. According to the *Derbyshire Times*, her posters in the commercial design section were 'a revelation of the ability of the youthful artist who this year had sold about £30 worth of her designs to various firms'. The previous July, she had won second prize in the competition for a design for an emblem for the Chester and Wrexham Trustees Savings Bank, and one of her designs had been accepted by the LMS railway. After college, she was employed in the design department of Robinson & Sons. When she married Marshall Haslam in 1939, the report of the wedding said that she gave up her job on marriage, like many women at that time.

Minnie Wheatcroft 1897-1973

Minnie Dawson was born in 1897. She lived with her parents, Mary and Tom Simpson Dawson, a labourer, at 9 Saltergate. They moved to 11 Saltergate, presumably when the adjacent Shakespeare Inn was rebuilt in 1906. In 1915, she married Matthew Henry Wheatcroft. Known as Harry, he was well known in Chesterfield, where he had worked for Shentalls Fruitiers since he had been 14.

He enlisted into the Sherwood Foresters in October 1914. After training, he was posted to Ireland. In February 1917, he was transferred to France, and he had only been there for two months when he was injured. Unfortunately, he lay where he fell for six hours before he could be rescued. He was wounded in the head, right arm, and right foot. Both limbs had to be amputated. Minnie received a letter, dictated by him, telling her not to worry because he would soon be home in England, but complications set in. At the beginning of May, Minnie received a letter saying that he had died.

The Women's Army Auxiliary Corps WAAC (known as the Queen Mary's Army Auxiliary Corps 1918-21) was established, and began recruiting in 1917. Women joining the WAAC acted as cooks, clerical workers, signallers, store-keepers, domestic staff, drivers, and waitresses. Minnie enlisted and was stationed at Rouxmes Camp near Dieppe. She spent the rest of the war in France driving ambulances. While she was there, she collected autographs of some of the soldiers. The album survived and is now in the National Army Museum, London. After the war she returned to live with her mother.

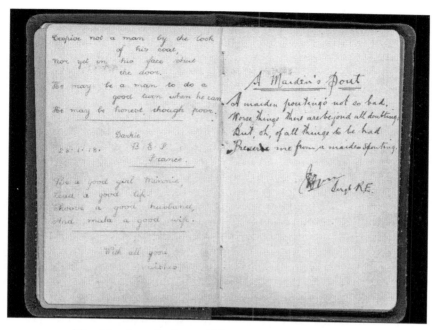

Minnie's autograph album with her name on the left hand page.

In 1939, when Trooper C. Roberts was on leave, he reported to the *Derbyshire Times* that, when he was billeted in a village in France, he met a French woman, who, on learning that he was from Chesterfield, asked him to look Minnie up, as she had been billeted in the same village in WWI. Trooper Roberts was able to put the pair in touch again. A further coincidence was that Minnie's husband had served under Trooper Robert's father.

When WWII began, Minnie joined the WVS, and was also an air raid warden. The Duke of Kent visited Chesterfield in March 1941 and inspected the Civil Defence contingent. He met co-workers, Minnie Wheatcroft and Annie Hindle. They told him that they had seen terrible sights when they had been sent to Manchester and Sheffield when the cities were bombed. On a lighter note, Minnie was responsible for organising entertainments for wounded soldiers.

Minnie died on 16 March 1973.

Other women known to have joined the WAAC, were Annie Turner, who worked in the Borough Accountant's Department and Maud Wood, daughter of J. H. Wood, licensee of the Wheatsheaf Hotel. Together, they sailed for France in September 1917. Maud married Lt L.P. Steenkamp of the ASC (South Africans) of Rhodesia at Chesterfield Parish Church in September 1919. The couple met in France and intended to live in South Africa.

Not everyone could adapt to life in the WAAC. Julia Ann Lynch applied to enlist in February 1918, saying that she was 20 years of age, whereas in fact she was only 18. She later withdrew her application, as she had heard the rumours about the immoral conduct of members of the WAAC (see Violet Markham). She proceeded with the application in August, and collected her uniform on 9 September. Five days later, she went absent without leave. Brought before the Borough Court as an absentee, she said that she didn't want to go back because she didn't get enough to eat. However, she did return, but, in December, she was in trouble again for neglecting to obey orders. She had two days leave over Christmas, and this possibly unsettled her again, and she was discharged on compassionate grounds in February 1919.

Helen Mary Wilcockson 1906-2002

Helen Mary Sylvester was the daughter of John Ernest Sylvester, who was a Brewer's Cashier, and his wife Amelia. She trained as a teacher. In 1929, she married Eric Keith Wilcockson whose family were builders' merchants in the town. After living in Chesterfield, the couple moved to Wingerworth. They had one daughter.

Helen was the first Chesterfield woman member of the Civil Air Guard to qualify for her pilot's 'A' certificate. She was interviewed for the *Derbyshire Times* of 9 June 1939.

In 1938, Helen heard a talk on the wireless by a woman who was giving a talk about the Civil Air Guard, which was formed in July 1938 with the intention of training pilots, who might then enlist in the Royal Air Force or the Fleet Air Arm. Women were placed in Class C with the thought that some of them might join the Air Transport Auxiliary, perform special duties in military or civil aviation, or move to non-aviation war duties.

She started training at Tollerton airport (now Nottingham City Airport) at the beginning of 1939. On 29 March after having been up with an instructor for a total of nine-and-a-quarter hours, she made her first solo flight, which lasted for five minutes, making a circuit at a height of 600 feet.

Helen took her 'A' certificate on an Avro Cadet after 15 hours training. The test included a solo flight of 3 hours 15 minutes. According to this certificate of competency, she was now qualified to fly 'all types of land planes'. She thoroughly enjoyed her training, but was not keen on the stalls and spins which she thought an ordeal – 'A stall is sickening when the machine is out of control until you have regained flying speed'

Her biggest thrill was her first cross country flight, which didn't go according to plan. According to an interview by a reporter from the *Derbyshire Times*:

'I took a pilot with me, and we planned to go to Chesterfield: a place I was very keen to fly over. The new Town Hall, by the way is an absolute godsend to pilots. It shows up more than the Crooked Spire and you can see it miles away. We got here safely and then I piloted the machine over our house at Wingerworth where we did a bit of stunting. We set our course for returning, and up till now we had been doing it very professionally with a compass and map. Unfortunately however, my companion's map blew away so I handed him mine while I continued to fly by the compass. He kept saying we were miles off course, and he made me turn the plane, which I felt was in the wrong direction.

After flying for half an hour, he announced that we were hopelessly lost, and we were due home in 10 minutes. We flew over a little town and I tried to read the name of the station but could not see it. Then I took off in the direction I felt we ought to go, and after a few minutes we came over another town which I found to be Burton, owing to the name being on the top of the gasometer – a great idea. So I followed the railway track home to Nottingham and on landing we found that the inside of the compass had fallen out!'

Her husband Eric, who had complete confidence in her, hoped to be her first passenger and her daughter was also keen to go up with her mother.

At the time of the air test, Helen was described as a housewife. During the war, she joined the WVS and went to London during the Blitz, where she helped feed rescue and demolition workers. After the war, she became a member of Wingerworth Parish Council, a JP for Derbyshire and Chairman of Chesterfield County Court.

Helen died at Buxton in 2002.

Marie Wilkes 1859-1910 and Alice Stevens 1862-193-?

Many Chesterfield girls have cause to be grateful to Miss Wilkes and Miss Stevens founders of Chesterfield Girls' High School.

Marie Louise Wilkes was born in Nottingham in 1859, the

eldest daughter of John Wilkes, a banker's clerk, and his wife Elizabeth. She was educated at Lockedy School, a private school, and Nottingham High School, after it opened in 1875, where she took the Cambridge Local Examinations in French and German. In the course of time, she became an assistant mistress at the school, Afterwards, she held a similar post at Liverpool High School until 1882, when she went to India to take up a post at the Diocesan College at Mussorie in one of the hill stations. Five years later, she returned to England to be an assistant mistress at Edgbaston Church College, Birmingham. Lodging in the same house was Alice Stevens.

Alice Stevens was born at Southampton in 1862, the daughter of a builder, Samuel Stevens, and his wife Fanny. In 1871, aged nine, she was at a school run by two governesses at Melcombe Regis (Weymouth) in Dorset. In 1881, she was a Public School Teacher boarding in Greenwich, so it is likely that she was a teacher at Blackheath High School, which opened in 1880. When the couple decided to open a school in Chesterfield, the advertisements for the opening of the Chesterfield Girls' High School described Miss Stevens as being late of Newnham College, Cambridge.

In 1871, Newnham was a house in which young ladies could reside whilst attending lectures in Cambridge, before they were able to take degrees. Newnham Hall opened in 1875. Alice studied there from 1879-1880. The course of studies she undertook would have prepared her to become a teacher. The fees for a term were £20, which suggests that her family was moderately well off.

In August 1892, an advertisement appeared in the *Derbyshire Times* saying that the kindergarten and school of Miss Walton was being re-opened at East Bank, as the High School for Girls. The school was the continuation of a kindergarten begun, in

1887, by Miss Walton as a private establishment in the Congregational schoolroom on Marsden Street. It outgrew the premises, as the girls stayed on and the boys left at the age of seven – usually for the Grammar School. The Misses Wilkes and Stevens lived at the Shrubberies on Newbold Road, sadly now demolished.

The school opened with just 30 pupils, but, by 1904, there were 99 girls and 13 small boys attending. Then, the school was under the direction of its lady principals and a committee, including representatives of the School Board (later Chesterfield Borough Council Education Committee), the Grammar School, and the County Council. Therefore, the school had powerful backers, unlike Holywell House School, which opened shortly afterwards, primarily as a boarding school with day students, and which closed in 1901 following an outbreak of diphtheria. Although the High School was a private school, there were 17 scholarships – five paid for by the Grammar School and the rest funded by the County Council. Miss Wilkes and Miss Stevens each received a salary of £60 p.a. plus board and lodging with a bonus if the school made a profit. Unfortunately, the popularity of the school caused problems, as it was short of space, and there was not have enough income to pay for additional teachers, which resulted in girls having to go elsewhere to finish their education (see the Robinson sisters). In 1904, it was recommended that the school should be brought under local authority control and a new building erected on a bigger site. The County Council took over the running of the school in 1906, and plans were passed for a new building on the opposite side of Sheffield Road. Miss Wilkes was the headmistress and Miss Stevens the second mistress.

The foundation stone for the new building was laid in 1909, but Miss Wilkes was sadly unable to benefit from the vastly improved accommodation of the new building. She had been in ill health since the beginning of the summer in 1910, when she underwent an operation for cancer. This was successful and the patient made such progress that hopes were entertained for her recovery. However, they were not realised and she was compelled to resign at the beginning of the Christmas term to enter a nursing home in Sheffield, where she died on 10 December 1910. A memorial service was held at Chesterfield Parish Church. The funeral took place at Sheffield General Cemetery.

The new building opened in September 1911. Miss Stevens relinquished her post as second mistress in 1912 due to ill health to become the lady housekeeper of the school.

Alice Stevens took an active part in social activities in Chesterfield. She was a member of Chesterfield Students' Association and, in 1905, she gave a talk about her impressions of Florence to those attending the Oxford University Extension Lectures. She was a member of the Chesterfield Women's Liberal Association and the Congregational Literary Social Union. She was also an active member, and member of the committee, of the Chesterfield branch of the NUWSS. After the death of Miss Wilkes, Alice left the Shrubberies to live in a smaller house on Fairfield Road.

In spring 1914, she retired to go to live with her brother in Bournemouth. She attended a school speech day in 1935, and probably died shortly afterwards.

The school song/hymn was *Pioneers* by Walt Whitman. It is made up of lines from *Pioneers O Pioneers*. In 1892 (the same year that the school opened), the Pioneer Club was opened in London. The name was said to be inspired by Whitman and his poem *Pioneers O Pioneers*. The qualities for membership required that the candidate 'shall have taken an active and personal interest in the various movements for Women's Social, Education, and Political advancement'. As Miss Wilkes and Miss Stevens were living in Wolverhampton, they might not have been members, but they would have met the qualifications for membership. It is feasible that they might have chosen *Pioneers* for the school song. The pioneers in this case were females taking advantage of new opportunities however the words weren't set to music until 1925, so it's not certain when the song was adopted.

The names of Wilkes and Stevens lived on in the school until it closed in 1991, as two of the houses were named Wilkes and Stevens.

Susannah Williams 1873-1956

Susannah was born at Ollerton, Nottinghamshire, the second daughter of George Ward and his wife Susannah. George was a gamekeeper on the estate of Earl Manvers at Thoresby Hall. In 1876, the family was living at Bishopsbourne in Kent. By 1891, George and family had moved to Wingerworth leaving behind his daughters Jane and Susannah, who were parlour maids at the home of Charles Beck, a major in the 13th Lancers, living at Cheriton, near Shorncliffe Army Camp, Kent. In 1893, Susannah married Rupert Williams, a sergeant in the 3rd Dragoon Guards. Their first daughter, Ruperta Alice, was born in the barracks at Canterbury; a second daughter Amy was born at Shorncliffe, but, by the time a son Rupert Daniel was born, Rupert senior had left the army and was working as a clerk for Derbyshire County Council. The family was living at Spital, although Ruperta and Amy spent some time living with their grandparents at Wingerworth. Rupert died in 1910. He was buried at Calow Church, where Susannah was a Sunday school teacher. A year later, Susannah's daughters were working as book binders for Wilfred Edmunds Ltd. publishers of the *Derbyshire Times*, whilst Rupert was still at school.

During the war, Susannah was employed as a forewoman at Staveley Coal and Iron Company. After the war, she was, for some time, housekeeper for Charles Markham, and, after his death, at other local properties, where her experience as a parlour maid would have been useful.

Susannah Williams and her grandson's motor bike.

Having been a widow for 46 years, she died, aged 84, in 1956. The funeral service was held at St Leonard's Mission, where she had attended the Women's Bible Class, before she was interred at Spital Cemetery. She left three children, seven grandchildren, and seven great grandchildren.

Susannah's stint at Staveley Coal and Iron Company involved walking daily from Spital to Staveley, organising her teams of girls, who had replaced the men, and then walking home again after a long day at work. She was one of a small army of women who were employed as munition workers during the war to manufacture a range of products. At Proctors on Park Road, 30 women were employed in manufacturing ammunition boxes; in the potteries, rum and jam jars were made; 50 young ladies were working at Markham Works; there were 100 at Bryan Donkin works; 20 at Plowright's; 100 worked at Chesterfield Manufacturing Company, where they were engaged in manufacturing fuels for gas stoves; at Robinsons & Sons, they were making dressings (Wheatbridge) and cardboard boxes (Holmebrook); the Patent Electric Shot-Firing Company was a big employer of women to manufacture fuses and detonators for Mills bombs and at Eyres they undertook joinery. Elsewhere they made mosquito nets, and were employed in the engine sheds at Staveley and Barrow Hill, drove trams and acted as railway porters. Sadly, little is known of their experiences and, after the war, many of the jobs disappeared as the men returned home.

Workers at the Patent Electric Shot Firing Company

Mary Woodhead 1904-1978

Mary was the only daughter of John Frederick Woodhead of Woodhead's grocers and his wife Mary Helen. She had three brothers.

She was closely involved with the work of the NSPCC–first as a member of the Ladies' Committee and then as Honorary Secretary. She was also a member of the Invalid and Children's Committee as part of the Borough Welfare Committee.

On the outbreak of WWII, Mary became very involved in the WVS, which, in 1936, had been established nationally. She became the officer in charge of the Chesterfield and District Car Pool, and, on one occasion, she travelled to London for ten days to take over the car pool there, so that the officer could have a holiday.

Together with Greta Walker, she organised the Kit Bag Club in Chesterfield. The experience gained there must have come in useful when she joined three other members of the WVS to open a canteen for members of the Merchant Navy, once the port of Cherbourg had been retaken. Conditions were somewhat primitive and they had to sleep on straw mattresses. After three months at Cherbourg, she moved to Rouen to a club where conditions were very different. Together with a lady from Worksop, she was billeted in a luxurious flat belonging to a French couple at the American HQ, where the only drinks available were champagne and brandy. The countryside around Rouen was desolate, the roads were in a dreadful state, and there were no bridges over the Seine. After a spell of leave back in England, she was based in Germany, in Hamm and Dortmund, before driving a WVS mobile library for the soldiers – the first to arrive on the Continent – in the battered area of the

Ruhr. Afterwards, she opened the first forces canteen in Cherbourg.

Flower bed in Queen's Park to celebrate the 40th anniversary of the WRVS in Chesterfield, possibly the work of Catherine Parry.

After the war, Mary continued to work with the WVS. In 1950, she was appointed deputy county organiser and, in June 1968, county organiser. She was one of the members who set up 'Meals on Wheels' in the county followed by 'Darby and Joan' clubs and luncheon clubs. In 1967, Mary received an M.B.E. to add to the B.E.M. received in 1954 for her services to the WVS (which became the WRVS in 1966).

She also organised the catering for Army Cadet camps around the county, and for the Mountain Rescue teams, particularly in the potholing districts.

Although she retired in 1974, Mary continued with, 'Meals on Wheels' in the Dronfield area until her death in January 1978.

Amy Wright 1825-1893

In 1818, John Wright was a stone mason on St Mary's Gate. He and his wife Elizabeth had three sons – Thomas born about 1800, Robert (1809), and Henry (1815). By 1835, John Wright and Son (probably Henry) were in business on Hollis Lane, and Thomas Wright and his wife Hannah lived on Lordsmill Street. Henry, who was also a stone mason, later lived on Durrant Green.

Thomas had two sons, John (1820) and William Sherwood (1826), and a daughter Anne (1825). After Thomas died, William, a stone mason, lived with his mother and Anne on Lordsmill Street. In 1851, Henry's family was living on Newbold Road and his eldest daughter Amy was a dress maker. Henry appears to have been more successful than Thomas, as he was employing two masons and two labourers. His son Thomas was an apprentice mason.

William Sherwood Wright married his cousin Amy Wright at St Peter and Paul, Sheffield (now the Cathedral) on 28 July 1851. The address for the pair was Castle Green in Sheffield, and banns had been read. A witness was William's sister Anne. Why they married in Sheffield is a mystery – perhaps Amy's father was opposed to the wedding; also Amy was pregnant with their first child. In 1853, William Wright, stone mason, engraver on stone and bricklayer, announced in the *Derbyshire Times* that he was taking over premises on St Mary's Gate opposite the Parish Church. This suggests that the business was expanding. By 1861, he had moved to the bigger premises at 9 Beetwell Street. The house, which still stands, dates back to the late 16th and early 17th centuries and is a Grade II* listed building; there was also a long yard to the rear and outbuildings. William was also a grocer and provision dealer.

The couple had nine children. With the exception of Eleanor

Sherwood, who died aged seven, and Margaret Ann aged 13, all reached adulthood. It was fortunate that William's sister Anne lived not far away, earning her living as a shopkeeper, and she would have been able to offer support.

In 1870, William carried out restoration work at the west end of the Parish Church before turning his attention to the chancel at the east end, where he restored the stonework and replaced the roof.

William died on 9 May 1872, a few days before his 47th birthday. Amy was left with seven children to look after, the youngest being just three. After sorting out the finances of the business, Amy was faced with the choice of selling the business or running it herself, as her eldest son John was only 16-years-old. In August, she placed advertisements in the *Derbyshire Times* 'respectfully informing the public that her late husband's business would continue'. She had first-class workmen in her employment, and was described as being an engraver of tombstones, monuments etc, and dealer in chimney and drain pipes, Roman and Portland cement, plaster of Paris, fire bricks, and all kinds of building materials.

In December 1875, it was announced that a limited liability company had been formed with the intention of providing a club for the local gentry resident in the East Derbyshire Parliamentary Division to be known as the East Derbyshire Club. The building on Saltergate was to include rooms to be leased in perpetuity to the Scarsdale Lodge of Freemasons. A tender of £2,730 3s 6d from Amy Wright was accepted. It is somewhat surprising that such a powerful group of men, building a club for men, should accept the tender from a firm of builders run by a woman. The building sold to the Freemasons when the East Derbyshire Club was wound up in 1925.

Masonic Hall, Saltergate

In 1879, Amy's son, John, was a stone mason, and his brother, William, was advertising himself as a teacher of the pianoforte and harmonium. In the 1881 cencus, he was described as a musician. However, in 1891, he was once more a stone mason.

In 1883, a newspaper article about the new St James's Church in Temple Normanton described the pulpit of stone, with Derbyshire marble columns to the arcaded portion and the font, which formed a fine feature at the west end of the church, which was also of moulded stone with a band of conventional foliage carved round the upper part of the bowl; both this and the pulpit were the work of Mrs Amy Wright of Chesterfield, from the designs of the architects. However, the carving was done by John Holdin of Sheffield.

In 1890, John married and moved to Hollis Lane. Two years later, Amy's daughter, Mary Hannah, died aged 32. Amy was left at home with just two sons, and one daughter. In 1893, Amy

Wright, builder and monumental mason, placed a series of advertisements in the *Derbyshire Times*, advertising her work as a monumental mason, and the existence of the building department. Possibly trade was slow because of the depression in the town at the time (see Annie King).

Amy died 1 June 1893, and was buried with her daughter Mary at Spital Cemetery; they were joined by Ann Wright, William Sherwood's sister who died 15 May 1900. A fortnight later, Amy's executors offered for sale a portion of furniture and household effects, as John took over the business and he, and his wife, Hannah, moved to Beetwell Street. Nothing more is heard of William – evidently he had had enough of being a stone mason.

Spital Cemetery was opened in 1857, and William Sherwood Wright was ideally placed for the manufacture of the headstones and monuments. However, in the early years, with only one person in a grave, there would have been few headstones erected, and it was his son, John Thomas Wright, who was responsible for many of the grave markers in the cemetery.

Index

Art	31-2, 107
Bacon, Katie	1-4, 88
Baden-Powell, Olave	4-7
Board of Guardians	34, 56, 100
Bond, Emma Louise	7-11
Borough Council Elections	8-10, 17, 61, 80
Borough Welfare Committee	8, 59, 119
Brampton/ Old Brampton	45, 50, 66-7, 84, 86
Carruthers, Violet	see Markham, Violet
Castle, Baroness Barbara	11-3
Chesterfield and North Derbyshire Hospital	18, 28, 56
	See also Royal Hospital
Chesterfield Civic Guild	8, 46, 48, 59, 103
Chesterfield Girls' High School	13-4, 31, 39, 79, 100, 104, 112-6
	See also St Helena School
Communist Party of Great Britain	39, 93
Cowley, Marjorie	13-5
Eastwood, Blanche	15-8
Elder Yard Chapel	7, 10, 65, 101-2
First Aid Nursing Yeomanry (FANY)	81-2
Fletcher, Anne Veronica	18-9
Fletcher, Mary Ellen	18-21
Foljambe, Isabel	21-2
Football	27-30, 63
Freeman, Elizabeth	23-4
Frith, Susannah	25-7

Girl Guides	18, 6-7, 32, 57, 77
Green, Florrie	27-30
Guildhall School of Music and Drama	54, 84, 86
Hanson, Phyllis	31-2
Harrison, Catherine	34
Harrison, Charlotte	33-5
Harrison, Rhoda Lucy	34-6
Hawes, Hilda	36-8
Heathfield , Betty	38-40
Independent Chapel	16 See also United Reformed Church
Jenkins, Dame Jennifer	40-2
John, Gwen	see Jones, Gladys
Johnson, Sarah	42-6
Jones, Gladys	48-50
Jones, Winifred	46-50
King, Annie	50-3
Kit Bag Club	84, 104, 109
Lynch, Julia Ann	110
Magistrate	18, 57, 81, 106, 112
Mallinson, Susan	54-5
Markham, Margaret	56-7
Markham, Violet	16-7, 57-64, 79, 89.
Mayor/ Mayoress	16, 57, 62, 81
Miller, Emma	65-9
Murray, Lady Mary	69-73
Music	1-4, 32, 86-8
National Union of Women's Suffrage Societies(NUWSS)	47, 79, 90-1
Newbold	96-9
Newstead, Katherine	see Katie, Bacon

Nurses and nursing   13-5, 18-21, 34, 36-8, 79, 81-3, 102-4

Parry, Catherine   73-4

Performing Arts   1-4, 33, 48-50, 54-8, 80, 84-8

Queen Alexandra's Imperial Nursing Service (QAIMNSR)   18-21, 35

Ragged School   19, 50-3

Religion   21-2, 25-7, 50-3, 75-7

Renishaw Hall   5, 96, 98

Richardson, Baroness Kathleen   75-7

Roberts, Hannah   77-9

Robinson, Cecile   79, 81-4

Robinson, Dorothy   79, 83-4

Robinson, Florence   64, 79-81, 84

Robinson and Sons   28-30, 38, 63, 79-80, 83-4, 93, 107, 118

Royal Hospital   18, 36, 56, 91, 102
See also Chesterfield and North Derbyshire Hospital

(The) Settlement   8, 63-4, 81, 93, 107

Shentall, Susan   84-6

Simon, Elizabeth   4, 86-8

Smith, Hannah   88-9

Smith, Jessie   48, 59, 79, 89-91

Smith, Rose   91-5

Spital Cemetery   17-9, 33, 102, 117, 124

St Helena School   54, 75
See also Chesterfield Girls' High School

Stevens, Alice   90, 112-6

Stovin, Margaret   95-9

Suffragettes, Suffragists   23-4, 46-8, 60, 79, 90

Swanwick, Mary   99-102

Tattersall, Rhoda	102-4
Territorial Forces Nursing Service (TFNS)	19, 36-8
Turner, Annie	110
United Reformed Church	75, 77
University Extension Lectures	92, 89, 100, 115
Upcott, Janet	62
Walker, Greta	104-7, 119
Webster, Doreen	107
Wheatcroft, Minnie	108-110
Whittington	36-8, 91-2, 101-2
Wilcockson, Helen, Mary	110-2
Wilkes, Marie Louise	112-6
Williams, Susannah	116-7
Women's Army Auxiliary Corps (WAAC)	60, 108-10
Worker's Educational Association (WEA)	92, 104
Women's Social and Political Union (WSPU)	23, 47, 80
Women's Voluntary Service (WVS)	84, 106, 109, 112, 119-120
Wood, Maud	110
Woodhead, Mary	105, 119-120,
Wright, Amy	121-4
World War I (WWI)	8, 14-5, 18-20, 30, 34-8, 60, 79-82, 108-9, 117-8
World War II (WWII)	36, 60, 82-4, 102-3, 109-110, 112, 119